Voyages to the Virginia Colonies

Born in 1533, Richard Hakluyt entered the Church and became Archdeacon of Westminster in 1603, before abandoning that life to take up a lectureship in cartography at Oxford. He was appointed geographical advisor to the East India Company several years later, and was one of the original members of the Virginia Company, the full inception and history of which is the subject of his *Voyages to the Virginia Colonies*. He was also the co-author, with Sir Walter Raleigh, of the famous treatise on British Naval Supremacy, *The Principal Navigations, Voyages and Discoveries of the English Nation (1589–1600)*.

This new edition was modernised, and is here reprinted with a new Introduction, by the respected historian A. L. Rowse. Not only is this the first opportunity for modern readers to have access to a fascinating historical work, but it also gives an extraordinary and unparalleled insight into the world of Elizabethan dominance.

A. L. Rowse is the author of many books on the subject of Elizabethan England, including *Eminent Elizabethans*, *Christopher Marlowe*, *Elizabethans and America*, *Expansion of Elizabethan England* and the highly-acclaimed *The England of Elizabeth*.

The cover shows a 'Map of Virginia', drawn by John Smith, 1624

Voyages to the Virginia Colonies

by Richard Hakluyt

a modern version, with an Introduction, by
A. L. Rowse

Century
London Melbourne Auckland Johannesburg

This edition first published in 1986 by The Folio Society

First paperback edition published in 1986 by Century, an imprint of
Century Hutchinson Ltd, Brookmount House, 62–65 Chandos Place,
London WC2N 4NW

Century Hutchinson Group South Africa (Pty) Ltd
PO Box 337, Bergvlei, 2012 South Africa

Century Hutchinson Australia Pty Ltd
PO Box 496, 16–22 Church Street, Hawthorn, Victoria 3122, Australia

Century Hutchinson New Zealand Ltd
PO Box 40–086, Glenfield, Auckland 10, New Zealand

ISBN 0 7126 9574 5

Photoset by Rowland Phototypesetting Ltd
Bury St Edmunds, Suffolk
Printed in Great Britain by
Richard Clay Ltd, Bungay, Suffolk

Contents

INTRODUCTION

HAKLUYT AND NORTH AMERICA

The consequences of Richard Hakluyt's work have established him as one of the most significant of all Elizabethans. He was a man of vision, and in several fields; in his case what he envisaged came off and bore fruit. In the first place Renaissance geography was revolutionised by the progressive discovery of the New World. Quite young, Hakluyt introduced the new knowledge and propagated it at Oxford during the sixteen years he was at Christ Church – my old College – 1570–1586. He then went to Paris as secretary to the ambassador, and used the opportunity to collect all the information he could, particularly about French voyages and settlements in Canada and Florida. Hakluyt was specially interested in North America and became the chief propagandist for English settlement there.

We must remember an important factor in the miraculous Elizabethan achievement – it is that England, on the north-western edge of Europe, was small and backward: it was the speed with which the Elizabethans caught up that was the miracle. We may compare Shakespeare's achievement in drama with Hakluyt's in the realm of geography, navigation, settlement across the Atlantic. They were contemporary: Hakluyt was born in 1552, Shakespeare in 1564; both died in 1616, and Hakluyt was buried in Westminster Abbey. Shakespeare read in Hakluyt's works, as several indications reveal, including the reference to the finest and most authoritative of his maps, 'the new map with the augmentation of the Indies', both East and West (i.e. America), in *Twelfth Night.*

Hakluyt was inspired first by the idea of making all the

new information about the world available to the English, and secondly by the opportunity of awakening them to earlier English achievements at sea, going right back to the voyages of the original Anglo-Saxons in Northern Europe. While in Paris Hakluyt realised all the more acutely the failure of the English to put themselves on the map, so to speak, in print and writing compared with other peoples. He had a proper admiration for the magnificent Spanish and Portuguese achievements. He had instigated John Florio, Shakespeare's later acquaintance (and Southampton's Italian tutor), to make his translation from the leading Italian geographers, Ramusio's Voyages. In the magical 1580s – when everything came together at once – he had published his first collection, *Divers Voyages*, and we find him getting regular leaves of absence to go to London or Bristol to collect material or take down information from the lips of sea-captains and write up their voyages.

In 1585 he himself had Laudonnière's account of his Florida voyage published in Paris. In the year of the Armada Hakluyt was over in England seeing to the printing of his classic *Principal Navigations* (published the next year 1589), which has been well described as 'the epic of the English nation'. It was the right historic moment to produce it. He was rewarded with the rectory of Wetheringsett in Suffolk, and later with prebends in Bristol cathedral and Westminster Abbey – for the Elizabethans did not fail to reward those who had notable initiative and put it at the service of the nation. Notice that each was a good location for his mission, collecting maritime material – his Suffolk rectory convenient for the East Anglian coast, Bristol and Westminster obvious for his purposes. He went on and on collecting, transcribing, translating and setting others to work, editing and writing – until in 1598–1600 he published the second edition of his great work, much fuller and bigger, and more critically edited. For his was a critical mind, not credulous, like so many Elizabethans. Nor did he cease to work: he went on accumulating, leaving a considerable quantity of material for Purchas to include in his continuation of this side of Hakluyt's work.

For it was one side of it, not the whole. No less important was his dual rôle as propagandist for English settlement and as adviser to the group of those who were prepared to give their energies, their fortunes and their lives to effecting it. We have a double reason for appreciating the importance of this today. I once quoted to Churchill the penetrating remarks of Bismarck: 'What is the decisive fact in the modern world? – The fact that North America speaks English.' (Churchill replied: 'Yes, I have often quoted it myself.') Twice in our lifetime that fact has saved Britain from the overmighty Continental power of Germany.

The Elizabethans looked ahead. When Spain was dominant in Central and South America, Hakluyt looked to North America as the proper sphere for English-speaking settlement. It was Spain's power in the New World, with the silver and gold that made it so profitable to her, that gave her the means to interfere in other countries all over Western Europe. The future of the English peoples depended on their getting a foothold in North America. Spain would have kept everybody else out if possible: already in 1572 she had sent a reconnaissance expedition to the Chesapeake – and had destroyed the French colony in Florida with a thorough massacre.

In 1584 we find Hakluyt in London preparing his 'Discourse on Western Planting' for Raleigh to present to the Queen. Hakluyt argued that Spain's actual hold in the New World was more limited in its area than people realised; that territories not already occupied by other Christian powers were open to settlement. England was 'so far from want of people' that an outlet for surplus population was desirable, besides the advantages of increasing the country's wealth by trade, especially in commodities complementary to the home market. Hakluyt was approved of by the Queen and her chief ministers, Walsingham, Secretary of State, and Lord Treasurer Burghley.

Hakluyt was active in advising those who were prepared to risk life and fortune in what was not to become a national enterprise until the foundation of the Virginia Company, after the peace with Spain, in 1606. The lead was taken by Sir Humphrey Gilbert, half-brother of Walter Raleigh who had become a favourite with the Queen. The Gilberts and Raleighs had temperaments in common: impulsive and temerarious men of action, soldiers by training, they were also well-educated Oxford men (like Hakluyt), intellectuals, on whom ideas acted like wine.

Gilbert had long been interested in the obsessive subject with Elizabethans – how to find a passage either by north-west or north-east, around the land-masses of America or Siberia, that would give England a route to the riches of trade with the Far East that was not under the control of Spain. We find this theme as a counterpoint to settlement in North America – the settlers were always on the look-out for river-routes that gave promise of an opening to the west. I suggest that at the turning point of Gilbert's Voyage to Newfoundland, when he insisted on a course west north-west against better advice, and the *Delight* was lost, he may have had the hope of such an outlet. Gilbert was an inveterate optimist; the Queen did not invest in his prime voyage of 1583, saying that he was 'not of good hap by sea'. However, she sent him a jewel by Raleigh, 'an anchor guided by a lady'. It did not save him, the event proved her right.

So we begin with the voyage of 1583, which, in spite of failure and loss – the good ship *Delight* with all Gilbert's notes and charts, the ore he had hopefully collected, and the sacrifice of his own life – nevertheless was the event that set things going, under the Letters Patents he had been granted for settlement. These, it must be realised, were an act of state, a governmental decision in favour of settlement, mobilised however by private enterprise and resources, which in the long run proved insufficient. Gilbert claimed formal possession of Newfoundland on behalf of the Queen, and by authority of his patent – hence Newfoundland's traditional ranking as first of the colonies that came in time to form an empire.

We should like to know more about Gilbert's backers, apart from the family. Raleigh's contribution was to have been the *Bark Raleigh*, but the crew refused to go on the voyage, to his anger and disgust. Sir Philip Sidney was very much interested and got a vast hypothetical grant of land. He wished to follow up Gilbert's voyage, 'whereunto Mr Hakluyt hath served for a very good trumpet'; but the Queen refused him permission to go. He died in the Netherlands instead.

The account of Gilbert's return home in the little *Squirrel* and the last sight of him with a book in hand – 'We are as near God by sea as by land' – the sudden going out of the ship's lantern, overwhelmed by a big sea, is famous, written by Edward Hayes, a gentleman, presumably of the West Country from some indications in his narrative. Nevertheless, for all his tributes to Gilbert, his initiative and gifts, one detects a note of criticism of his rashness, the risks he was prepared to take – exactly what the Queen thought, who had known him for years – he had been her personal servant when she was princess.

When Gilbert's loss became known, Raleigh immediately got the transference of the patent to himself before it ran out. It may be to him that we owe the imaginative touch of the name 'Virginia' for the whole of North America open to English settlement; the name had the political implication that the Queen was interested; that this was to be the English sphere. Next year 1584 Raleigh despatched a reconnaissance voyage to the southern coast of North America, as more promising than the bleak prospects of Newfoundland, which someone described as 'a wilderness in a sea swarming with fish'. Raleigh's bark made a successful reconnaissance of the coast south of the Chesapeake and we have Arthur Barlow's charming account of it, or his account of its charms. This has an element of promotional literature in its enthusiasm, naturally enough – but indeed the southern approach and coast offered better prospects than Newfoundland (always excepting fish).

This was the preliminary to the First Colony of 1585–6, the most important voyage of all until the ultimate foundation of Jamestown in 1607, of which it was the precursor. Much thought and preparation went into this venture, in which the leading spirit was Raleigh. He had the advice of Hakluyt at command, the backing of Walsingham, who invested in the enterprise, and that of the Queen. She would not, however, let Raleigh go on it; his place was taken by his cousin Sir Richard Grenville. Hakluyt gives us various accounts from which we see the picture and, with a little imagination, can grasp its significance. We have the journal of Grenville's flagship, the *Tiger*, for its record of external events; the letter of Ralph Lane reporting to Hakluyt, and his Discourse on the proceedings of the colony on Roanoke Island. Most important, we have the cardinal work of Thomas Hariot, *A Brief and True Report of the new found land of Virginia*, which is published here together with John White's maps and drawings of the fauna and flora, and his vivid rendering of the Indians and their way of life.

It is hardly possible to exaggerate the importance of these works or of the experience which they record, for upon the knowledge they gathered the later permanent settlement was based. Hariot's brief book – founded upon a larger collection of notes and observations – excited great attention in Europe: it was translated into Latin and had no less than seventeen editions in the next quarter of a century. For the remainder of the century it remained the prime authority as to conditions of life, climate, inhabitants, products, potentialities and prospects in North America. When the great publisher, Theodore de Bry, came to London, Hakluyt suggested to him his classic publication, *America*; and drew his attention to White's drawings which were engraved for it, while Hariot wrote the Latin captions. Hakluyt translated them.

Both Hariot (1560–1621) and White (dates unknown) are of great importance in any history of the first colonists. Both are less well known than they deserve. What is known about John White and his marvellous drawings is set out at the end of this introduction. Of Hariot, one can reasonably say that, all things considered, he may be regarded as the foremost scientific mind among Elizabethans – as against a type like John Dee, whose considerable knowledge was clouded with a great deal of speculative nonsense and credulity. Hariot had the prime qualification of a modern scientist of believing nothing without evidence. He is the first algebraist of the age, along with Viete, making original contributions to the development of mathematics. As an astronomer, he used optic instruments and made significant observations contemporaneously with, and appreciated by, Galileo. He was physicist and meteorologist; and we see from his Report he was a good way on to being an anthropologist. In the Elizabethan manner he was no departmentalised specialist, he took all science for his parish; but, heterodox in his views, he published little: he dared not say all that he thought – even so, he was the subject of suspicion and attack.

Sometimes Hariot's Report tells us more, sometimes White's maps and drawing. We must remember that together they constitute the core of a larger monument conceived by the scientific genius of Hariot – splendid illustrated work on Virginia, i.e. English North America, which was never realised because of the loss, suffered by both of them, of material which would have gone to the making of it.

Hariot had a proper belief in the future prospects of the country. 'Why may we not then look in good hope from the inner parts of more and greater plenty, as well of other things as of those which we have already discovered? Unto the Spaniards happened the like in discovering the main of the West Indies [i.e. the mainland from the West Indies]'. How right the great scientist was, with his speculative mind, when we think today of the North American continent providing foodstuffs for most of the world!

Thomas Hariot – an Oxford man, like Hakluyt, Gilbert, Raleigh and Sidney – was the most eminent of Elizabethan mathematicians, and a ranging scientific mind no less interested in astronomy, physics, meteorology and anthropology. He was Raleigh's intellectual adviser. John White, cartographer, is regarded as the first in the long line of English water-colourists; it is fairly certain, from his close association with Raleigh, that it was he who captained further voyages sent out by Raleigh. Thomas Cavendish was the provost-marshal on the expedition, and immediately on his return put in hand preparations for the voyage which made him the second circumnavigator of the globe after Drake.

Drake was familiar with the Virginia project and, on his way back from his campaign in the Caribbean which announced open war with Spain, brought reinforcements for the colony, when Grenville's promised supply was late in arriving. All plans were disrupted, however, by a hurricane which swept down on them, and forced ships to run clear to sea. In something like a panic the colonists closed with Drake's offer to transport them home. In the hurry to get away many of Hariot's notes and observations and White's drawings were cast away by the sailors. When Grenville's supply ships arrived, the colony had gone.

We have a brief account, from the pen of Hakluyt himself, of Raleigh's attempts to supply the colonists. Shortly after their 'departing out of this paradise of the world' his ship arrived but, not finding them, brought back their intended provisions. A fortnight after, Grenville arrived with three ships; finding Roanoke deserted and hearing no news of the colonies, he left fifteen men there with provisions for a couple of years.

The detailed happenings, the story in itself, we may leave to the original narratives we present from Hakluyt. But we should make the strategic background clear. The Spanish posts in Florida were intended to deny the eastern coast of North America to foreigners, and later a Spanish expedition to the Chesapeake swept the Bay thoroughly, and would have liquidated an English colony if they had found one. The advantage of Roanoke Island behind the North Carolina Banks was that it was not visible from the coast; the approach to it was hazardous through narrow inlets and shifting shoals. It was in fact a hideout, and it took the Spaniards a long time to find out where the English effort was located. But, by the same token, there was no good harbour, and the danger to ships was forcibly brought home to all by the hurricane which dissipated the First Colony. Subsequent efforts were intended for the Chesapeake, where ultimately a permanent settlement was made.

In 1587 a further major effort took shape – the Second or Lost Colony, which has left its mark in American folklore, if not on the land. Raleigh sent out three ships, with another complement of a hundred or so colonists, under the command of John White. Their instructions were to plant the colony in Chesapeake Bay, but the sailors insisted on landing them on Roanoke, which they knew. We have John White's account of this. It is evident that he was not a tough enough man to command obedience. Both Grenville and his deputy, Ralph Lane, are criticised as harsh disciplinarians, but clearly one needed to be tough to keep an Elizabethan crew in order, let alone command a successful voyage.

On the other hand there are several indications that Lane's

harshness to the Indians – notably his killing of the chief Wingina – was disapproved of. It went clean contrary to Hakluyt's insistence on maintaining good relations, difficult as that may have been with acute competition for food supplies. We may see the story of what Lane regarded as a conspiracy as the initial step in the long and tragic dichotomy between the white and the red men for possession of the (not wholly) virgin continent. And perhaps I may suggest, more precisely, that it gives us the explanation of the total disappearance of the subsequent colonists without trace – while making their way, it has been thought, through trackless wilderness to the Chesapeake.

At home this year, 1587, Hakluyt brought out his edition of Peter Martyr's standard work on the New World, with a dedication to Raleigh. Either this year or the next, evidently in consequence of residing in Suffolk, Hakluyt married Douglas Cavendish, a relation of the circumnavigator – amusing to see how the geographer co-ordinated his interests. Two years later Raleigh made Hakluyt one of the nineteen grantees named in his charter for 'the city of Raleigh in Virginia'.

He did not entirely desist from his efforts, for all that he, Grenville, Drake and everybody had other things to do in the great crisis of Armada year. Grenville was in fact gathering ships at Bideford for a third weighty expedition, when it was countermanded and he was ordered to take his ships round to Plymouth to serve against the gathering Armada. Only two little barks, the *Brave* and the *Roe*, were permitted to sail; but in the war-time conditions in the western approaches, chasing and being chased, they were forced back. We have again an account from John White, who was in command.

It has been asked why nothing was done to carry aid and sustenance to the colonists in 1589 – if any were left. The answer is obvious: both Raleigh and Grenville were up to their eyes with their affairs in Ireland, where they had large land-grants in Munster to attend to, besides the chores assigned them at sea around the western coasts. Drake was absorbed in the large Lisbon expedition – the English reply to the Armada. As we have seen, Hakluyt was absorbed in seeing his great work through the press.

In 1590 a last expedition was sent out, again under John

White's command, whose account of it we have. He was no more effective than before, though he did get back to Roanoke. There he found the sad relics of former occupation: 'about the place many of my things spoiled and broken and my books torn from the covers, the frames of some of my pictures and maps rotten and spoiled with rain . . . this could be no other but the deed of the savages, who had watched the departure of our men to Croatoan.' There was an indication in that word cut in capital letters on a tree that it was thither that the colonists of the Lost Colony had departed. White says that he intended to make for Croatoan to search for them, but a series of accidents to their anchors, and then the onset of bad weather, prevented them. Once more he proved ineffective – corroboration, perhaps, that the artistic temperament rarely goes with command.

Raleigh was criticised, notably by Francis Bason, for failing to come to the rescue of his colonists – we do not imagine that they survived long, though the Indians of Croatoan were supposed to be friendly. But Raleigh was understandably discouraged; he had spent large sums (he said, £40,000) and immense labours on these enterprises – with no return, unlike the treasure Spain garnered from Mexico and Peru. In 1592 occurred his disgrace with the Queen⋆ – after which he turned his attention to Guiana as bearing promise of gold, an Eldorado.

Relics of Raleigh's obsessive imagination are to be found, like fossils, in his verse:

> *To seek new worlds for gold, for praise, for glory . . .*

> *My hopes clean out of sight with forcèd wind*
> *To kingdoms strange, to lands far off addressed . . .*

We find that the cedars of Barlow's and Hariot's reports had left their impressions:

> *On highest mountains where those cedars grew*
> *Against whose banks the troubled ocean beat,*

⋆ For a full account of this v. my *Raleigh and the Throckmortons.*

And were the marks to find thy hopèd port
Into a soil far off themselves remove . . .

Hakluyt was by no means discouraged, though permanent
settlement in North America awaited the end of the war with
Spain, for which it was in part waged. At the peace in 1604
it was assumed that the principle of the open door had been
won and North America was open to English settlement.
Hakluyt continued his work, as active as ever, and encouraging others. He himself wrote up an account of George Drake's
voyage to the island of Ramea, off the Newfoundland
coast. We may regard this as a sequel to Gilbert's pioneering
voyage of 1583; as we may think of the extrusion of the
Spaniards and Portuguese from the Newfoundland fishery
from 1585 as a consquence of it. A more admirable consequence was the series of John Davis's remarkable voyages into
higher latitudes than reached by any, up into Davis Strait,
on the way to a North-West Passage. (Davis was a tenant
of the Gilberts in the parish of Stoke Gabriel in Devon.)
We have seen that Raleigh's Virginia efforts flowed directly
from Gilbert's original impulse. Naturally, because of
his close association with them, Hakluyt's accounts of the
North American Voyages – particularly for the hopeful
decade, 1578–1588 – are the fullest and best informed; this
is where his prime interest lay, and these are what we now
present.
We have seen that Hakluyt was regarded with favour by
the Queen and her ministers, though the lesson of all these
efforts was that the resources of private individuals – Raleigh's
came ultimately from the Queen – were insufficient for the
task ahead: it would need the continuing flow of City money
organised in joint-stock form. On Walsingham's death the
Cecils took his place in backing Hakluyt. Lord Burghley
encouraged his interest in the St Lawrence and Canada; he
collected the maps we see still in the library at Hatfield. To
his son as Secretary of State Hakluyt dedicated his vastly
improved *Principal Navigations* in three volumes in 1599.
Hakluyt was impressed by Cecil's knowledge and judgment,
as well he might be, and once more he made acknowledgment

to Richard Staper of the Clothworkers' Company* (and client of Simon Forman) for constant support.

In 1596 Hakluyt was translating material about South America, particularly the Amazon and Guiana, the new direction of Raleigh's interest, and he encouraged the scholarly (but drunken) John Pory to translate the history of Africa. He was in touch with the eminent Dutch geographers, van Meteren, in preparation for Barentz's voyages to the northeast, supplying information regarding that of Pett and Jackman in 1580. In 1600 he was involved in aiding the foundation of the East India Company – the Dutch had drawn upon English accounts of the East Indies in founding their prosperous Company. Next year he dedicated *The Discovery of the World*, from the Portuguese of Galvão, to Cecil; he had already helped Molyneux to make his famous globes, which incorporated Edward Wright's world-map, the best to date.

With the peace of 1604 the country was at last free to push forward settlement in North America in good earnest, both in south and north Virginia, the latter of which came to be known as New England. The Virginia Company of 1606 was to deal with both areas, the London branch with southern settlement, Plymouth with the northern. Hakluyt was named third among the grantees under the Company's charter, and he subscribed for two shares. Drayton's splendid Ode for the intended venture properly included praise for 'industrious Hakluyt', while sea-captains and navigators expressed their appreciation of all that he had done by naming after him headlands and peaks and forelands in far-off places. He was well provided for; he got the chaplaincy of the Savoy from Cecil's patronage, and the rectory of Gedney in Lincolnshire, perhaps from the same source. It was a charming thought of the East India Company to send out to its factors in 1611 Hakluyt's great work 'to recreate their spirits with variety of history'.

To recreate our spirits, as well as for instruction, we need to read Hakluyt in modern English. Fundamentally, Hakluyt's English *is* modern. *Littérateurs*, when they write about Eliza-

---

* For Richard Staper v. my *Simon Forman: Sex and Society in Shakespeare's Age*.

bethan prose, think of it as elaborate and fanciful, rhetorical and laboured. They are thinking of literary works like Sidney's *Arcadia*, Lyly's *Euphues*, or Hooker's *Laws of Ecclesiastical Polity* – though the prose of Shakespeare's plays is not like that. These people – Virginia Woolf and Lytton Strachey, for example – are not well read, as an historian must be, in ordinary, everyday Elizabethan language, in the way people talked, the thousands of letters they wrote, the documents they left.

Hakluyt's narratives are like that, the speech of plain folk, direct and easy to follow, with occasional flashes of fancy or phrases of natural beauty, like Barlow's, approaching Virginia after weeks at sea, the land smelling 'so sweetly, as if we had been in the midst of some delicate garden, abounding with all kind of odoriferous flowers'. Hakluyt's English can be appreciated all the better for being rendered simply, not altered, in modern spelling, punctuation and paragraphing. The same is true for all Elizabethan English, including Shakespeare; there is no point in retaining rebarbative spelling – ye olde Tudor Tea-schoppe forms – merely creating difficulty for the reader and adding nothing of value. Disembarrassed of uncouth spelling, a modern text brings out the fascination of the stories in themselves, unencumbered.

One exception may be made to this rule – Spenser's spelling, for he was deliberately archaic and attached importance to the form in which he presented his dream-world. Hakluyt's was not a dream-world, but the everyday world of common experience, of action and endeavour, of lives lived and lost at sea, of exploring new lands, the excitement of new peoples and their ways, unknown birds and beasts, fishes and flowers. It is well known that Shakespeare's exquisite play, *The Tempest*, was sparked off by William Strachey's account of the hurricane which overtook the flagship of the Virginia Voyage of 1609, but there are sufficient indications that behind the play, as behind the voyage, was reading much to the point in Hakluyt.

John White and his drawings

John White's water-colour drawings of North America – in particular of the areas the Elizabethans called Virginia, now the coastal strip of North Carolina – are of surpassing interest and important from several points of view. First, for detailed and visual information about North America, the Indians of the south-east, their habits, way of life and subsistence. Secondly, for geographical knowledge, in particular cartography, and subsidiarily ethnography; and no less for natural history and botany, his rendering of the flora and fauna of the region. Thirdly, there is his importance as an artist, as the first of many excellent British water-colour painters. Lastly, there is the strange and romantic story of the drawings themselves, which were so very nearly lost. To appreciate John White's drawings properly we have to see them in perspective, both historical and artistic.

It was only after an extraordinarily belated interval that John White began to be taken notice of for himself and his drawings estimated at their true worth. In his own time they were only known at all widely through De Bry's engravings of them for his magnificent *America* – and then De Bry got all the credit for them. In the eighteenth century appeared the one person who appreciated White's work at its true worth, and did his best to collect and preserve it: a remarkable man in his own right, the great physician and naturalist, Hans Sloane. Mark Catesby copied a few of White's originals for his superbly illustrated *Natural History of Carolina*. The original drawings were later sold for 14 guineas to Lord Charlemont, in whose possession they remained until they were auctioned in 1865. The warehouse in which they were stored caught fire, and the drawings narrowly escaped destruction. The volume containing them was charred around the edges; but worse damage came from its saturation in water. This had the effect of prettily off-setting some drawings on the opposite page; but naturally it detracted from the brilliance of the original colouring. We see from this chapter of accidents how providential their survival has been!

Having emerged into the light of day, albeit slightly damaged, they were bought by the scholarly Henry Stevens of Vermont. Even he could arouse no interest for their purchase in America – in 1865 the United States, so recently disunited, had other things to think about. Next year the great and discerning Panizzi bought them for the British Museum for a mere £236 5s. At last after the Second World War, justice was at length done them by the splendid and scholarly volumes edited by Paul Hulton and D. B. Quinn, 1964, the standard work which must remain the basis for any further investigation: a limited edition and highly expensive however, not easy to procure. Next year, the drawings – worked up from sketches made on the spot – voyaged for the first time to the United States, where they had been inspired and the sketches made, to be exhibited in North Carolina, in Washington, and at the opulent Pierpont Morgan library in New York. Now, to celebrate the Quartercentenary of the First Virginia Colony, The Folio Society is reproducing these remarkable drawings, together with the text that they were intended to illustrate, Hariot's *Brief and True Report of the new found land of Virginia*, together with other major accounts of this extraordinary period of pioneering discovery.

We know little about John White's background, other than that he probably came from the West Country, which was the breeding ground for the great explorers of the Elizabethan age. Walter Raleigh was his patron and it was Raleigh who sent out the First Colony of 1585–6, which was intended for permanent settlement. Though that hope was in the end frustrated – and had to wait another twenty years to be fulfilled with Jamestown in 1607 – nevertheless the First Colony was of prime importance. From it flowed all the rest: experience of American climate and natural conditions, of life alongside Indians, natural products and potentialities of subsistence. All this and more, including the narrative of events, and incorporated in Thomas Hariot's *Brief and True Report of the new found land of Virginia*, and backed up by the visual evidence of John White's drawings.

Raleigh naturally wished to lead this historic mission himself, into which he had put so much effort and so many resources. But at this stage of his somewhat tortuous relationship with that maiden lady, the Queen, she could not spare him from her side on so dangerous a journey. In his place Raleigh deputed his cousin, Sir Richard Grenville, as leader, later to become the hero of the last fight of the *Revenge*. It is fairly clear that in the subsequent attempt to settle a Virginia colony with John White as governor, he was not sufficiently authoritative to get his wishes executed. The gentlemanly artist, though personally spirited and courageous, lacked a tough streak in dealing with others; his drawings show that he was sympathetic and sensitive. Grenville was neither; however, he carried through his mission successfully and planted the colony: it was not his fault that it failed.

Most of John White's surviving drawings were the product of the first Roanoke Colony, during the years 1585–1586. These were made for Sir Richard Grenville's expedition which had left Plymouth on 9 April 1585, with seven vessels. (Sir Richard's own narrative of the voyage, and an anonymous account of this first attempt at planting a colony in Roanoke, follow in Chapter 8.)

The little fleet took the now familiar route to the West Indies, the northern route, the coast of what was to become New England, being much less known and more dangerous, as Gilbert found. Early in May they were off Puerto Rico and anchored in what is now Tallaboa Bay, on the island of St John, White gives us a complete picture of the camp, fortifications, men in disciplined formation, the general on horseback, the three-masted *Tiger* in the foreground. We are reminded how self-sufficient such an Elizabethan expedition had to be – furnace, smiths, carpenters for eventualities. They landed for fresh water, scouring the country for supplies and commodities with which to stock the colony ahead: hogs, sows, cattle, horses, foodstuffs and plants which they hoped to set and grow. Evidently it was from this sojourn in the West Indies that White sketched his pineapple, mamee apple and plaintains (bananas).

Then, out of the Florida Channel – John White sketching dolphins and flying fish on the way – for the great venture, the American mainland, protected by the Carolina Banks, with their shifting shoals and islands through which it was necessary to find an inlet, and, if possible, a harbour. We have pen-and-ink sketch maps of the coast showing roughly what it was like then; but we must remember that it has greatly changed since: islands linked up, inlets extinguished etc. On the mainland, opposite Roanoke, the largest island, was the Indian village of Pomeioc, with Secoton further away to the south. On 11 July Grenville set out with the pinnace and some small boats to explore the mainland, White busy sketching. Next day they visited the palisaded village of Pomeioc, of which White gives us a complete and most informative picture. The drawings provide important material for anthropologists, like all White's drawings of Indian life; the character of the housing – several interiors with sleeping benches are shown, with no divisions into rooms.

Meanwhile, they rowed up the shallow Pamlico river to the village of Secoton, where they were well entertained. Here too, White gives us a remarkably detailed rendering of the place and its inhabitants.

After their return from exploring the mainland, three weeks were employed in settling the colonists on Roanoke, before Grenville, having accomplished his mission, left for England on 25 August. Ten days later he came to Plymouth where Raleigh was awaiting him, and 'courteously received by divers of his worshipful friends'.

For the extent of the vast territory lying there to be opened up we must turn to the large-scale map White built up from various sources – the south-eastern coast of North America all the way from Florida Keys to Chesapeake Bay, the most easterly point being Cape Hatteras. The whole southern coast is given French names; they were evidently drawn from French sources, and corroborate the availability of information from the extinguished colony in Florida, and White's contact with Jacques Le Moyne, its illustrator. When we come to White's smaller-scale map of the coast and territory explored from their base, we see how excellent his work and Hariot's observations were in detail. In addition to the information White gives us as to the immediate region of sounds and rivers within the Banks, he depicts the entrance to Chesapeake Bay as far as the debouching of the James and York rivers into it. Two Indian villages are named – Chesapeake and Skioac, a little way from its southern shore. This is important evidence of their exploration as far as that, for Chesapeake Bay was to become the venue of permanent settlement when Roanoke efforts failed.

Where Hariot was able to penetrate some way into the Indian mind, White gives us their external appearance, dress, activities and gestures. It is here, when we come to their habits, commodities and so on, that the co-ordination of White and Hariot is most eloquent. Hariot describes their houses as White depicts them, 'made of small poles made fast at the top in round form after the manner used in many arbours in our gardens of England'. White also gives us details of interior arrangements and dress. We have a picture of an Indian in grand get-up and war-paint, holding a bow as tall as himself with a roll of arrows carried on his thigh. He is stuck with feathers in his head, hung with necklaces, body painted all over, an animal's tail hanging between his legs.

White gives us several paintings of Indian women. One is of a Pomeioc chief's wife, holding a large gourd, with a daughter of eight or ten years carrying a doll in European dress – a present from the colonists? A similar chief's wife has her baby clambering up her back.

More interesting and exotic still is the portrait of a wizard or magician. White calls him 'the flyer': he has a bird attached to his head, so presumably he is supposed to be a bird; legs and arms are in movement, as if casting a spell.

Between harvests the Indians lived mostly by fishing and hunting, collecting nuts and fruits. We have a vivid drawing of 'the manner of their fishing': a canoe – so-named, and the name itself is from the West Indies – made of a long hollowed out tree trunk; one man at either end, one punting and the other with a drag pole to catch the fish; the boat filled with large silvery fish; a couple seated at a fire in the middle, cooking. We have a separate picture of 'the broiling of their fish over the flame of fire': a couple of fish upon a framed grill, sticks burning underneath.

We have numerous drawings of fish, remarkable in colouring, and mostly new to English eyes, including the 'remora' which thoroughly intrigued the Elizabethans. Its common name was the 'sucking fish', and ancient folklore – carried into the Renaissance by Pliny – held that it could stay the course of a ship to which it attached itself: hence its name *remora*, meaning delay. We are given a magnificent full-page drawing of a land crab and another of two types of hermit-crabs. The drawings of the turtles are splendid, with every detail of appearance to satisfy a zoologist. In addition there are depictions of the iguana and the alligator, birds such as the flamingo, the frigate bird, and other native American species. There are studies of West Indian fireflies, a gadfly, a couple of scorpions, and the swallow-tail butterfly with its exquisite markings and pigmentation.

Though we unfortunately know so little about White, his work was known to the growing group of naturalists who belonged to the scientific movement characteristic of the age, though it is immeasurably less known than its literature. Some of his plant drawings no longer exist in the originals; but we have a fine full-page drawing of a pineapple, another of a round mamee-apple; one of a banana, with a sliced section showing the fruit and another of bunches to show how bananas grow on the stalk.

The end of the first colony came unexpectedly, precipitated by a tornado. Grenville was on his way with a supply ship and a few more men for the colony, but was overdue when Drake arrived from the full-scale attack on the West Indies, the opening attack of the war with Spain. Then the hurricane struck. When the storm subsided and it was possible to move, Drake offered the colony safe passage home and, unnerved and disenchanted, they were glad to take the offer. They were in such a hurry to go, 'that the most of all we had – with all our cards [i.e. maps], books and writings – were by the sailors cast overboard'.

The losses of these – Hariot's notes, White's maps and drawings – were irreparable.

Nonetheless, Raleigh, his backers and friends were by no means giving up. Grenville duly arrived at Roanoke to find the colony gone, and left fifteen men there to hold the fort at that outpost. For Raleigh's preparations were advancing for a Second Colony; not to take its place, but to settle more promisingly on the Chesapeake with its more open spaces and wider prospects. The scheme for the Second Colony, with White as governor, differed from the first. Raleigh was to be a kind of over-lord with his Letters-Patent from the Queen, but the 'City of Raleigh' envisaged was to be more self-subsistent and self-governing – individuals putting in their investment, to take up land later, White to be advised by twelve assistants. Such was the scheme on paper.

We have John White's own narrative of his transporting of

the Second Colony, written in the third person as governor. They made for the West Indies. We do not know whether the governor had any leisure for sketching this time, but we notice his continuing interest in the flora and fauna. 'We took five great turtles, some of them of such bigness that sixteen of our strongest men were tired with carrying one of them but from the seaside to our cabin . . .' His account of events comes further on in this volume.

John White was a remarkable man, in an age of remarkable men; Elizabethans were all-round men: Raleigh himself was soldier, sailor, politician, colonist, poet and historian, White was both an artist and a surveyor. His collaboration with Hariot was a fruitful one, their work dovetailing in to each other; we hear of no quarrels between them, they were happy in their work.

John White was not so accomplished or sophisticated an artist as Le Moyne in his figure drawing; in that lies his prime value – he is truer to the originals. His is the best record of North American Indian life, of the flora and fauna down to the insects – he made his contribution to zoology and to ethnology, as Hariot to anthropology and science in general. Their influence – Hariot's especially – was prodigious for the next century, and provided the basis of knowledge for permanent settlement twenty years later. Hariot was truly a herald of the new modern scientific mind, and thus of the modern world, while White set the model for the image of the American Indian which has prevailed even down to today.

1

SIR HUMPHREY GILBERT'S
NEWFOUNDLAND VOYAGE, 1583

A report of the voyage and success thereof, attempted in the year of our Lord 1583 by Sir Humphrey Gilbert, knight, with other gentlemen assisting him in that action, intended to discover and to plant Christian inhabitants in place convenient, upon those large and ample countries extended northward from the cape of Florida; lying under very temperate climes, esteemed fertile and rich in minerals, yet not in the actual possession of any Christian prince. Written by Edward Hayes, gentleman, and principal actor in the same voyage, who alone continued upto the end, and by God's special assistance returned home with his retinue safe and entire.

Many voyages have been intended, yet hitherto never any thoroughly accomplished by our nation of exact discovery into the bowels of those main, ample and vast countries, extended infinitely into the north from 30 degrees, or rather from 25 degrees of septentrional latitude. Neither has a right way been taken of planting a Christian habitation and regiment upon the same; as well may appear both by the little we yet do actually possess therein, and by our ignorance of the riches and secrets within those lands. Unto this day we know them chiefly by the travel and report of other nations; and most of the French, who albeit they can not challenge such right and interest unto the said countries as we, neither these many years have had opportunity nor means so great to discover and to plant (being vexed with the calamities of intestine wars) as we have had by the inestimable benefit of our long and happy peace. Yet have they both ways performed more, and had long since attained a sure possession and settled government of many provinces in those northerly parts of America, if their many attempts into those foreign and remote lands had not been impeached by their civil wars at home.

The first discovery of these coasts (never heard of before) was well begun by John Cabot the father, and Sebastian, his son, an Englishman born, who were the first finders out of all that great tract of land stretching from the cape of Florida unto those islands which we now call the Newfoundland. All which they brought and annexed unto the crown of England. Since when, if with like diligence the search of inland countries had been followed, as the discovery upon the coast, and out-parts thereof was performed by those two men, no doubt her Majesty's territories and revenue had been mightily enlarged and advanced by this day. And which is more: the seed of Christian religion had been sowed amongst those pagans, which by this time might have brought forth a most plentiful harvest and copious congregation of Christians. Which must be the chief intent of such as shall make any attempt that way; or else whatsoever is builded upon other foundations shall never obtain happy success nor continuance.

And although we can not precisely judge what have been the humours of men stirred up to great attempts of discovering and planting in those remote countries, yet the events do show that either God's cause has not been chiefly preferred by them, or else God had not permitted so abundant grace as the light of his word and knowledge of him to be yet revealed unto those infidels before the appointed time.

It seems probable by event of precedent attempts made by the Spaniards and French sundry times, that the countries lying north of Florida, God has reserved the same to be reduced unto Christian civility by the English nation. For not long after that Christopher Columbus had discovered the islands and continent of the West Indies for Spain, John and Sebastian Cabot made discovery also of the rest from Florida northwards to the behoof of England.

And whensoever afterwards the Spaniards (very prosperous in all their southern discoveries) did attempt any thing into Florida and those regions inclining towards the north, they proved most unhappy, and were at length discouraged utterly

by the hard and lamentable fortune of many both religious
and valiant in arms, endeavouring to bring those northerly
regions also under the Spanish jurisdiction. As if God had
prescribed limits unto the Spanish nation, which they might
not exceed – as by their own actions recorded may be aptly
gathered.

The French, as they can pretend less title unto these
northern parts than the Spaniard, by how much the Spaniard
made the first discovery of the same continent so far northward as unto Florida, and the French did but review that
before discovered by the English nation – usurping upon our
right, and imposing names upon countries, rivers, bays,
capes, or headlands, as if they had been the first finders of
those coasts. Which injury we offered not unto the Spaniards,
but left off to discover when we approached the Spanish
limits. Even so God has not hitherto permitted them to
establish a possession permanent upon another's right, notwithstanding their manifold attempts; in which the issue has
been no less tragical than that of the Spaniards, as by their
own reports is extant.

These considerations may help to suppress all fears rising
of hard events in attempts made this way by other nations;
as also of the heavy outcome and issue in the late enterprise
made by a worthy gentleman, our countryman, Sir Humphrey
Gilbert, knight, who was the first of our nation that carried
people to erect an habitation and government in those northerly countries of America. About which, albeit he had consumed much substance, and lost his life at last, his people also
perishing for the most part, yet the mystery thereof we must
leave unto God, and judge charitably both of the cause (which
was just in all pretence) and of the person. He was very
zealous in prosecuting the same, deserving honourable remembrance for his good mind, and expense of life in so
virtuous an enterprise. Nevertheless, lest any man should be
dismayed by example of other folks' calamity, and misdeem
that God does resist all attempts intended that way, I thought
good, so far as my self was an eye-witness, to deliver the
circumstances and manner of our proceedings in that action.
In which the gentleman was so unfortunately encumbered
with wants, and worse matched with many ill disposed

people, that his rare judgement and regiment premeditated for those affairs, was subjected to tolerate abuses, and in sundry extremities to hold on a course, more to uphold credit, than likely in his own opinion happily to succeed.

When first Sir Humphrey Gilbert undertook the western discovery of America, and had procured from her Majesty a very large commission to inhabit and possess at his choice all remote and heathen lands not in the actual possession of any Christian prince, the same commission exemplified with many privileges, such as in his discretion he might demand, very many gentlemen of good estimation drew unto him, to associate him in so commendable an enterprise. So that the preparation was expected to grow unto a puissant fleet, able to encounter a king's power by sea. Nevertheless, amongst a multitude of voluntary men, their dispositions were diverse, which bred a dispute, and made a division in the end, to the confusion of that attempt even before the same was begun. When the shipping was in a manner prepared, and men ready upon the coast to go aboard, at that time some broke consort, and followed courses degenerating from the voyage before pretended. Others failed of their promises contracted, and the greater number were dispersed, leaving the general with few of his assured friends, with whom he adventured to sea; where, having tasted of no less misfortune, he was shortly driven to retire home with the loss of a big ship, and (more to his grief) of a valiant gentleman, Miles Morgan.

Having buried only in preparation a great mass of substance, whereby his estate was impaired, his mind yet not dismayed, he continued his former purpose to revive this enterprise, good occasion serving. Upon which determination standing long, without means to satisfy his desire, at last he granted certain assignments out of his commission to sundry persons of mean ability, desiring the privilege of his grant, to plant and fortify in the north parts of America about the river of Canada. If God gave good success in the north parts (where then no matter of moment was expected) the same (he thought) would greatly advance the hope of the south, and be a furtherance unto his determination that way. And the worst that might happen in that course might be excused by the former supposition, that those north regions were of no regard. But chiefly a possession taken in any parcel of those heathen countries, by virtue of his grant, did invest him of territories extending every way two hundred leagues. This induced Sir Humphrey Gilbert to make those assignments. desiring greatly their expedition, because his commission did expire after six years, if in that space he had not gotten actual possession.

Time went away without any thing done by his assigns; insomuch that at last he must resolve himself to take a voyage in person, for more assurance to keep his patent in force, which then almost was expired, or within two years.

In furtherance of his determination, amongst others, Sir George Peckham, knight, showed himself very zealous to the action, greatly aiding him both by his advice and in the charge. Other gentlemen to their ability joined unto him, resolving to adventure their substance and lives in the same cause. Beginning their preparation from that time, both of shipping, munition, victual, men, and things requisite, some of them continued the charge two years complete without intermission. Such were the difficulties and cross accidents opposing these proceedings, which took not end in less than two years: many of which circumstances I will omit.

The last place of our assembly, before we left the coast of England, was in Cawsand Bay near unto Plymouth; then resolved to put unto the sea with shipping and provision, such as we had, before our store yet remaining, but chiefly the time and season of the year, were too far spent. Nevertheless it seemed first very doubtful by what way to shape our course, and to begin our intended discovery, either from the south northward, or from the north southward.

The first, that is, beginning south, without all controversy was the likeliest, wherein we were assured to have commodity of the current, which from the cape of Florida set northward. This would have furthered greatly our navigation, discovering from the foresaid cape along towards Cape Breton, and all those lands lying to the north.

Also the year being far spent, and arrived to the month of June, we were not to spend time in northerly courses, where we should be surprised with timely winter, but to covet the south, which we had space enough then to have attained.

There we might with less detriment have wintered that season, being more mild and short in the south than in the north where winter is both long and rigorous.

These and other like reasons alleged in favour of the southern course first to be taken, to the contrary was inferred. Forasmuch as both our victuals and many other needful provisions were diminished and left insufficient for so long a voyage, and for the wintering of so many men, we ought to shape a course most likely to minister supply. And that was to take the Newfoundland in our way, which was but seven hundred leagues from our English coast. Where being usually at that time of the year, until the end of August, a multitude of ships repairing thither for fish, we should be relieved abundantly and with many necessaries, which after the fishing ended, they might well spare, and freely impart unto us.

Not staying long upon that Newfoundland coast, we might proceed southward, and follow still the sun, until we arrived at places more temperate to our content.

By which reasons we were the rather induced to follow this northerly course, obeying unto necessity, which must be supplied. Otherwise, we doubted that sudden approach of winter, bringing with it continual fog, and thick mists, tempest and rage of weather. Also contrariety of currents descending from the cape of Florida unto Cape Breton and Cape Race would fall out to be great and irresistible impediments unto our further proceeding for that year, and compel us to winter in those north and cold regions.

Wherefore suppressing all objections to the contrary, we resolved to begin our course northward, and to follow directly as we might the trade way unto Newfoundland. From whence, after our refreshing and reparation of wants, we intended without delay to proceed into the south, not omitting any river or bay which in all that large tract of land appeared to our view worthy of search. Immediately we agreed upon the manner of our course and orders to be observed in our voyage; which were delivered in writing unto the captains and masters of every ship a copy.

Every ship had delivered two bullets or scrolls, the one sealed up in wax, the other left open: in both which were included several watch-words. That open, serving upon our own coast or the coast of Ireland; the other sealed, was promised on all hands not to be broken up until we should be clear of the Irish coast. This did serve until we arrived and met altogether in such harbours of the Newfoundland as were agreed for our rendezvous. The said watch-words being requisite to know our consorts whensoever by night, either by fortune of weather, our fleet dispered should come together again; or one should hail another; or if by ill watch and steerage one ship should chance to fall aboard of another in the dark.

The reason of the bullet sealed was to keep secret that watch-word while we were upon our own coast, lest any of the company stealing from the fleet might betray the same. This known to an enemy, he might board us by night without mistrust, having our own watch-word.

Our course agreed upon

The course first to be taken for the discovery is to bear directly to Cape Race, the most southerly cape of Newfoundland; and there to harbour ourselves either in Rogneux or Fermous, being the first places appointed for our rendezvous, and the next harbours unto the northward of Cape Race.

Beginning our course from Scilly, the nearest is by west south-west (if the wind serve) until such time as we have brought ourselves in the latitude of 43 or 44 degrees, because the ocean is subject much to southerly winds in June and July. Then to take traverse from 45 to 47 degrees of latitude, if we be enforced by contrary winds: and not to go to the northward of the height of 47 degrees of septentrional latitude by any means. But to do your endeavour to keep in the height of 46 degrees, so near as you can possibly, because Cape Race lieth about that height.

Orders thus determined, and promises mutually given to be observed, every man withdrew himself unto his charge, the anchors already weighed, and our ships under sail, having a soft gale of wind. We began our voyage upon Tuesday the eleventh day of June, in the year of our Lord 1583, having in our fleet (at our departure from Cawsand Bay) these ships.

1. The *Delight* alias The *George*, of burden 120 tons, was Admiral; in which went the general, and William Winter, captain in her and part owner, and Richard Clarke, master.

2. The *Bark Raleigh* set forth by Master Walter Raleigh, of the burden of 200 tons, was then Vice-admiral: in which went Master Butler, captain, and Robert Davis of Bristol, master.

3. The *Golden Hind*, of burden 40 tons, was then Rear-admiral: in which went Edward Hayes, captain and owner, and William Cox of Limehouse, master.

4. The *Swallow*, of burden 40 tons: in her was captain Maurice Browne.

5. The *Squirrel*, of burden 10 tons: in which went captain William Andrews, and one Cade, master.

We were in number in all about two hundred and sixty men. Among whom we had of every faculty good choice, as shipwrights, masons, carpenters, smiths, and such like, requisite to such an action; also mineral men and refiners. Besides, for solace of our people, and allurement of the savages, we were provided with music in good variety; not omitting the least toys, as morris dancers, hobby horse, and Maylike conceits to delight the savage people, whom we intended to win by all fair means possible. And to that end we were indifferently furnished with all petty haberdashery wares to barter with those simple people.

In this manner we set forward, departing out of Cawsand Bay the eleventh day of June being Tuesday; the weather and wind fair and good all day, but a great storm of thunder and wind fell the same night.

Thursday morning, when we hailed one another in the evening, they signified unto us out of the Vice-admiral, that both the captain, and very many of the men were fallen sick. And about midnight the Vice-admiral forsook us, notwithstanding we had the wind east, fair and good. But it was after credibly reported that they were infected with a contagious sickness, and arrived greatly distressed at Plymouth: the reason I could never understand. Sure I am, no cost was spared by their owner Master Raleigh in setting them forth.

By this time we were in 48 degrees of latitude, not a little grieved with the loss of the most puissant ship in our fleet. After those departure, the *Golden Hind* succeeded in the place of Vice-admiral, and removed her flag from the mizzen unto the foretop.

From Saturday the fifteenth of June until the twenty-eighth, which was upon a Friday, we never had fair day without fog or rain, and winds bad, much to the west north-west, whereby we were driven southward unto 41 degrees nearly.

About this time of the year the winds are commonly west towards the Newfoundland, keeping ordinarily within two points of west to the south or to the north. Whereby the course thither falls out to be long and tedious after June, which in March, April and May, has been performed out of England in twenty-two days and less. We had wind always so scant from west north-west, and from west south-west again, that our traverse was great, running south unto 41 degrees almost, and afterward north into 51 degrees.

Also we were encumbered with much fog and mists in manner palpable, in which we could not keep so well together, but were dissevered, losing the company of the *Swallow* and the *Squirrel* upon the twentieth day of July; whom we met again at several places upon the Newfoundland coast the third of August.

Saturday the twenty-seventh of July, we might descry not far from us, as it were mountains of ice driven upon the sea, being then in 50 degrees, which were carried southward to the weather of us. Whereby may be conjectured that some current sets that way from the north.

Before we come to Newfoundland about fifty leagues on this side, we pass the Banks, which are high grounds rising within the sea and under water; yet deep enough and without danger, being commonly not less than twenty-five and thirty fathom water upon them. The same (as it were some vein of mountains within the sea) do run along, and from the Newfoundland, beginning northward about 52 or 53 degrees of latitude, and do extend into the south infinitely. The breadth of this Bank is somewhere more, and somewhere less; but we found the same about ten leagues over, having sounded both on this side thereof, and the other toward Newfoundland, but found no ground with almost two hundred fathom of line, both before and after we had passed the Bank. The Portuguese, and French chiefly, have a notable trade of fishing upon this Bank, where are sometimes an hundred or more sails of ships: who commonly begin the fishing in April, and have ended by July. That fish is large, always wet, having land near to dry, and is called cod fish.

During the time of fishing, a man shall know without sounding when he is upon the Bank, by the incredible multitude of sea fowl hovering over the same, to prey upon the offals and garbage of fish thrown out by fishermen, and floating upon the sea.

Upon Tuesday the eleventh of June, we forsook the coast of England. So again Tuesday the thirtieth of July (seven weeks after) we got sight of land, being immediately embayed in the Grand Bay, or some other great bay. The certainty whereof we could not judge, so great haze and fog did hang upon the coast, as neither we might discern the land well, nor take the sun's height. But by our best computation we were then in 51 degrees of latitude.

Forsaking this bay and uncomfortable coast (nothing appearing unto us but hideous rocks and mountains, bare of trees, and void of any green herb) we followed the coast to the south, with weather fair and clear.

We had sight of an island named Penguin, of a fowl there breeding in abundance, almost incredible, which cannot fly, their wings not able to carry their body, being very large (not much less than a goose) and exceeding fat. Which the French men use to take without difficulty upon that island, and to barrel them up with salt. But for lingering of time we had made us there the like provision.

Trending this coast, we came to the island called Baccalaos, being not past two leagues from the main; to the south thereof lies Cape St Francis, five leagues distant from Baccalaos, between which goes in a great bay, by the vulgar sort called the bay of Conception. Here we met with the *Swallow* again, whom we had lost in the fog, and all her men altered into other apparel. It seemed their store was so amended that for joy and congratulation of our meeting, they spared not to cast up into the air and overboard, their caps and hats in good plenty. The captain, albeit himself was very honest and religious, yet was he not appointed of men to his humour and desert. They for the most part were such as had been by us surprised upon the narrow seas of England, being pirates, and had taken at that instant certain Frenchmen laden, one bark with wines, and another with salt. Both which we rescued, and took the man of war with all her men, which was the same ship now called the *Swallow*, following still their kind so oft, as (being separated from the general) they found opportunity to rob and spoil.

Thus after we had met with the *Swallow*, we held on our course southward, until we came against the harbour called St John, about five leagues from the former cape of St Francis. Before the entrance into the harbour, we found also the *Squirrel* lying at anchor. Whom the English merchants (that are always Admirals by turns over the fleets of fishermen within the same harbour) would not permit to enter into the harbour. Glad of so happy meeting both of the *Swallow* and frigate in one day (being Saturday the third of August) we made ready our fights, and prepared to enter the harbour, any resistance to the contrary notwithstanding. There were within, of all nations, to the number of thirty-six sails. But first the general dispatched a boat to give them knowledge of his coming for no ill intent, having commission from her Majesty for his voyage he had in hand. In the very entrance (which is but narrow, but above two butts length) the Admiral fell upon a rock on the larboard side by great oversight. But we found such readiness in the English merchants to help us in that danger, that without delay there were brought a number of boats, which towed off the ship.

Having taken place convenient in the road, we let fall anchors, the captains and masters repairing aboard our Admiral. Thither also came immediately the masters and owners of the fishing fleet of Englishmen, to understand the general's intent and cause of our arrival there. They were all satisfied when the general had showed his commission, and purpose to take possession of those lands to the behalf of the crown of England, requiring but their lawful aid for repairing of his fleet, and supply of some necessaries. So craving expedition of his demand, minding to proceed further south without long detention in those parts, he dismissed them. The merchants with their masters departed, they caused forthwith to be discharged all the great ordnance of their fleet in token of our welcome.

It was further determined that every ship of our fleet should deliver unto the merchants and masters a note of all their wants: the ships as well English as strangers, were taxed at an easy rate to make supply. Commissioners were appointed to go into other harbours adjoining (for our English merchants command all there) to levy our provision: whereunto the Portuguese (above other nations) did most willingly and liberally contribute. Insomuch as we were presented (above our allowance) with wines, marmalades, most fine rusk or biscuit, sweet oils and sundry delicacies. Also we wanted not of fresh salmons, trouts, lobsters and other fresh fish brought daily unto us. Moreover as the manner is in their fishing every week to choose their Admiral anew, or rather they succeed in orderly course, and have weekly their Admiral's feast solemnized; even so the general, captains and masters of our fleet were continually invited and feasted. After our wants and tedious passage through the Ocean, it seemed more acceptable and of greater contentation, by how much the same was unexpected in that desolate corner of the world: at other times of the year, wild beasts and birds have only the fruition of all those countries, which now seemed a place very populous and much frequented.

The next morning being Sunday and the fourth of August, the general and his company were brought on land by English merchants, who showed unto us their accustomed walks unto a place they call the Garden. But nothing appeared more than Nature itself without art: who confusedly hath brought forth roses abundantly, wild but odoriferous, and to sense very comfortable. Also the like plenty of raspberries, which do grow in every place.

Monday following, the general had his tent set up, who being accompanied with his own followers, summoned the merchants and masters, both English and strangers, to be present at his taking possession of those countries. Before whom openly was read and interpreted unto the strangers his commission. By virtue whereof he took possession in the same harbour of St John and two hundred leagues every way, invested the Queen's Majesty with the title and dignity thereof, had delivered unto him (after the custom of England) a rod and a turf of the same soil, entering possession also for him, his heirs and assigns for ever. And signified unto all men that from that time forward they should take the same land as a territory appertaining to the Queen of England, and himself authorised under her Majesty to possess and enjoy it. And to ordain laws for the government thereof, agreeable (so near as conveniently might by) unto the laws of England: under which all people coming thither hereafter, either to inhabit, or by way of traffic, should be subjected and governed. And especially at the same time for a beginning, he proposed and delivered three laws to be in force immediately. That is to say: the first for religion, which in public exercise should be according to the Church of England. The second for maintenance of her Majesty's right and possession of those territories: if any thing were attempted prejudicial, the party or parties offending should be adjudged and executed as in case of high treason, according to the laws of England. The third if any person should utter words sounding to the dishonour of her Majesty, he should lose his ears, and have his ship and goods confiscated.

These contents published, obedience was promised by general voice and consent of the multitude as well of Englishmen as strangers, praying for continuance of this possession and government begun. After this, the assembly was dismissed. And afterward were erected not far from that place the Arms of England engraven in lead, and fixed upon a pillar of wood. Yet further and actually to establish this possession taken in the right of Majesty, and to the behoof of Sir Humphrey Gilbert, knights, his heirs and assigns for ever, the general granted in fee farm divers parcels of land lying by the waterside, both in this harbour of St John, and elsewhere. This was to the owners a great commodity, being thereby assured (by their proper inheritance) of grounds convenient to dress and to dry their fish, whereof many times before they did fail, being prevented by them that came first into the harbour. For which grounds they did convenant to pay a certain rent and service unto Sir Humphrey Gilbert, his heirs or assigns for ever, and yearly to maintain possession of the same, by themselves or their assigns.

Now remained only to take in provision granted, according as every ship was taxed, which did fish upon the coast adjoining. In the meanwhile, the general appointed men unto their charge: some to repair and trim the ships, others to attend in gathering together our supply and provisions; others to search the commodities and singularities of the country to be found by sea or land, and to make relation unto the general what either themselves could know by their own travail and experience, or by good intelligence of Englishmen or strangers, who had longest frequented the same coast. Also some observed the elevation of the pole, and drew plots of the country exactly graded. And by that I could gather by each man's several relation, I have drawn a brief description of the Newfoundland, with the commodities by sea or land already made, and such also as are in possibility and great likelihood to be made. Nevertheless the cards and plots that were drawing, with the due gradation of the harbours, bays, and capes, did perish with the Admiral; wherefore in the description following, I must omit the particulars of such things.

A brief relation of the Newfoundland, and the commodities thereof

That which we do call the Newfoundland, and the Frenchman Baccalaos, is an island, or rather (after the opinion of some) it consists of sundry islands and broken lands, situated in the north regions of America, upon the gulf and entrance of the great river called St Lawrence in Canada. Into the which, navigation may be made both on the south and north side of this island. The land lies south and north, containing in length between three and four hundred miles, accounting from Cape Race (which is in 46 degrees 25 minutes) unto the Grand Bay in 52 degrees of northern latitude. The island round about has very many goodly bays and harbours, safe roads for ships, the like not to be found in any part of the known world.

The common opinion that is had of intemperature and extreme cold that should be in this country, as of some part it may be verified, namely the north – where I grant it is more cold than in countries of Europe, which are under the same elevation. Even so it cannot stand with reason and nature of the clime, that the south parts should be so intemperate as the brute has gone. For as the same do lie under the climates of Brittany, Anjou, Poitou in France, between 46 and 49 degrees, so can they not so much differ from the temperature of those countries. Unless upon the out-coast lying open unto the Ocean and sharp winds, it must indeed be subject to more cold, than further within the land, where the mountains are interposed, as walls and bulwarks, to defend and to resist the asperity and rigour of the sea and weather. Some hold opinion, that the Newfoundland might be the more subject to cold, by how much it lies high and near unto the middle region.

I am of opinion that the sun's reflection is much cooled, and cannot be so forcible in the Newfoundland, nor generally throughout America, as in Europe or Africa: by how much the sun in its diurnal course from east to west passes over (for the most part) land and sandy countries, before it arrived at the west of Europe or Africa, whereby its motion increases heat, with little or no qualification by moist vapours. Where, on the contrary it passes from Europe and Africa unto America over the Ocean; from whence it draws and carries with it abundance of moist vapours, which do qualify and enfeeble greatly the sun's reverberation upon this country chiefly of Newfoundland, being so much to the northward. Nevertheless the cold cannot be so intolerable under the latitude of 46, 47 and 48 (especially within land) that is should be uninhabitable, as some do suppose, seeing also there are very many people more to the north by a great deal.

And in these south parts there are certain beasts, ounces or leopards, and birds in like manner which in the summer we have seen, not heard of in countries of extreme and vehement coldness. Besides, in the months of June, July, August and September, the heat is somewhat more than in England at those seasons; so men remaining upon the south parts near unto Cape Race, until after first November, have not found the cold so extreme, nor much differing from the temperature of England. Those who have arrived there after November and December have found the snow exceeding deep; whereat no marvel, considering the ground upon the coast is rough and uneven, and the snow is driven into the places most declining. The like depth of snow happily shall not be found within land upon the plainer countries, which also are defended by the mountains, breaking off the violence of winds and weather. But admitting extraordinary cold in those south parts, above that with us here, it can not be so great as in Sweden, much less in Russia. Yet are the same countries very populous, and the rigour of cold is dispensed with by the commodity of stoves, warm clothing, meats and drinks. All which need not be wanting in the Newfoundland, if we had intent there to inhabit.

In the south parts we found no inhabitants, which by all likelihood have abandoned those coasts, the same being so much frequented by Christians. But in the north are savages altogether harmless. Touching the commodities of this country, serving either for sustenation of inhabitants, or for maintenance of traffic, it seems Nature has recompensed that only defect of some sharp cold, by many benefits: viz. with incredible quantity and variety of kinds of fish in the sea and fresh waters, as trout, salmon and other fish to us unknown. Also cod, which alone draws many nations thither, and is become the most famous fishing of the world. Abundance of whales, for which also is a very great trade in the bays of Placentia and the Grand Bay, where is made train-oils of the whale; herring the largest that have been heard of, and exceeding the Malstrond herring of Norway. But hitherto was never benefit taken of the herring fishing. There are sundry other fish very delicate, namely the bonito, lobsters, turbot, with others infinite not sought after; oysters having pearl but not orient in colour: I took it by reason they were not gathered in season.

Concerning the inland commodities, as well to be drawn from this land, as from the exceeding large countries adjoining: there is nothing which our east and northerly countries of Europe do yield, but the like also may be made in them as plentifully by time and industry. Namely, resin, pitch, tar, soapashes, dealboard, masts for ships, hides, furs, flax, hemp, corn, cables, cordage, linen-cloth, metals and many more. All which the countries will afford, and the soil is apt to yield. The trees for the most in those south parts, are fir trees, pine and cypress, all yielding gum and turpentine. Cherry trees bearing fruit no bigger than a small pea. Also pear trees, but fruitless. Other trees of some sorts to us unknown.

The soil along the coast is not deep of earth, bringing forth abundantly peas, small yet good feeding for cattle. Roses passing sweet, like unto our musk roses in form, raspberries, a berry which we call hurts, good and wholesome to eat. The grass does fat sheep in very short space, proved by English merchants which have carried sheep thither for fresh victual and had them raised exceeding fat in less than three weeks. Peas which our countrymen have sown in the time of May have come up fair, and been gathered in the beginning of August. Of which our general had a present acceptable for the rareness, being the first fruits coming up by art and industry in that desolate and dishabited land.

Lakes or pools of fresh water, both on the tops of mountains and in the valleys. In which are said to be mussels not unlike to have pearl, which I had put in trial, if by mischance falling unto me, I had not been prevented from that and other good experiments I was minded to make. Fowl both of water and land in great plenty and diversity. All kind of green fowl; others as big as bustards, yet not the same. A great white fowl called of some a gaunt.

Upon the land divers sorts of hawks, as falcons, and others by report; partridges most plentiful, larger than ours, gray and white of colour, and rough footed like doves, which our men after one flight did kill with cudgels, they were so fat and unable to fly. Birds some like blackbirds, linnets, canary birds, and others very small. Beasts of sundry kinds, red deer, buffalo or a beast, as it seems by the track and foot very large in manner of an ox. Bears, ounces or leopards, some greater and some lesser, wolves, foxes, which to the northward a little further are black, whose fur is esteemed in some countries of Europe very rich. Otters, beavers, martens. And in the opinion of most men that saw it, the general had brought unto him a sable alive, which he sent unto his brother Sir John

Gilbert, knight, of Devonshire: but it was never delivered, as after I understood. We could not observe the hundredth part of creatures in those uninhabited lands: which the more does aggravate the fault and foolish sloth in many of our nation, choosing rather to live indirectly and very miserably to live and die within this realm pestered with inhabitants, than to adventure as becomes men, to obtain an habitation in those remote lands, in which Nature very prodigally ministers unto men's endeavours, and for art to work upon.

For besides these already recounted and infinite more, the mountains generally make show of mineral substance: iron very common, lead, and somewhere copper. I will not aver of richer metals; albeit by the circumstances following, more than hope may be conceived thereof.

For amongst other charges given to inquire out the singularities of this country, the general was most curious in the search of metals, commanding the mineral man and refiner, especially to be diligent. The same was a German born, honest and religious, named Daniel, who after search brought at first some sort of ore, seeming rather to be iron than other metal. The next time he found ore, which with no small show of contentment he delivered unto the general, using protestation, that if silver were the thing which might satisfy the general and his followers, there it was, advising him to seek no further. The peril whereof he undertook upon his life (as dear unto him as the Crown of England unto her Majesty, that I may use his own words), if it fell not out accordingly.

Myself at this instant liker to die than to live, by a mischance, could not follow this confident opinion of our refiner to my own satisfaction; but afterward demanding our general's opinion therein, and to have some part of the ore, he replied: 'Content yourself, I have seen enough; and were it but to satisfy my private humour, I would proceed no further. The promise unto my friends, and necessity to bring also the south countries within compass of my patent near expired, as we have already done these north parts, do only persuade me further. And touching the ore, I have sent it aboard, whereof I would have no speech to be made so long as we remain within harbour. Here are Portuguese, Biscayans and Frenchmen not far off, from whom must be kept any bruit or muttering of such matter. When we are at sea proof shall be made: if it be to our desire, we may return the sooner hither again.' Whose answer I judged reasonable, and contenting me well: wherewith I will proceed to the rest of our voyage, which ended tragically.

While the better sort of us were seriously occupied in repairing our wants, and contriving of matters for the commodity of our voyage, others of another sort and disposition were plotting mischief. Some casting to steal away our shipping by night, watching opportunity by the general's and captains' lying on the shore: whose conspiracies discovered, they were prevented. Others drew together in company, and carried away out of the harbours adjoining, a ship laden with fish, setting the poor men on shore. A great many more of our people stole into the woods to hide themselves, attending time and means to return home by such shipping as daily departed from the coast. Some were sick of fluxes, and many dead; in brief, by one means or other our company was diminished, and many by the general licensed to return home. Insomuch as after we had reviewed our people, resolved to see an end of our voyage, we grew scant of men to furnish all our shipping. It seemed good therefore unto the general to leave the *Swallow* with such provision as might be spared for transporting home the sick people.

The captain of the *Delight* returned into England, in whose stead was appointed captain Maurice Browne, before captain of the *Swallow*. He brought with him into the *Delight* all his men of the *Swallow*, which before have been noted of outrage perpetrated upon fishermen there met at sea. The general made choice to go in his frigate the *Squirrel* (whereof the captain also was among them that returned into England), the same frigate being most convenient to discover upon the coast, and to search into every harbour or creek, which a great ship could not do.

Now having made ready our shipping, that is to say, the *Delight*, the *Golden Hind*, and the *Squirrel*, and put aboard our provision, which was wines, bread or rusk, fish wet and dry, sweet oils; besides many other, as marmalades, figs, lemons barrelled, and such like. Also we had other necessary provisions for trimming our ships, nets and lines to fish with, boats or pinnaces fit for discovery. In brief, we were supplied of our wants commodiously, as if we had been in a country or some city populous and plentiful of all things.

We departed from this harbour of St John's upon Tuesday the twentieth of August, which we found by exact observation to be in 47 degrees 40 minutes. And the next day by night we were at Cape Race, twenty-five leagues from the same harbour. This cape lies south south-west from St John's; it is a low land, being off from the cape about half a league; within the sea rises up a rock against the point of the cape, which thereby is easily known. It is in latitude 46 degrees 25 minutes. Under this cape we were becalmed a small time, during which we laid out hooks and lines to take cod, and drew in less than two hours, fish so large and in such abundance that many days after we fed upon no other provision.

From hence we shaped our course unto the island of Sablon, if conveniently it would so fall out, also directly to Cape Breton. Sablon lies to the seaward of Cape Breton about 25 leagues, whither we were determined to go upon intelligence we had of a Portuguese who was himself present when the Portuguese (above thirty years past) did put into the same island both oxen and swine to breed, which have since exceedingly multiplied. This seemed unto us very happy tidings, to have in an island lying so near unto the mainland, which we intended to plant upon, such store of cattle, whereby we might at all times conveniently be relieved of victual, and served of store for breeding.

In this course we trended along the coast, which from Cape Race stretches into the north-west, making a bay which some called Trépasse. Then it goes out again toward the west, and makes a point, which with Cape Race lies in manner east and west. But this point inclines to the north, to the west of which goes in the bay of Placentia. We sent men on land to take view of the soil along this coast, whereof they made good report, and some of them had will to be planted there. They saw peas growing in great abundance everywhere.

The distance between Cape Race and Cape Breton is 87 leagues. In which navigation we spent eight days, having many times the wind indifferent good; yet could we never attain sight of any land all that time, seeing we were hindered by the current. At last we fell into such flats and dangers, that hardly any of us escaped: where nevertheless we lost our Admiral with all the men and provision, not knowing certainly the place. Yet for inducing men of skill to make conjecture, by our course and way we held from Cape Race thither (that thereby the flats and dangers may be inserted in sea cards, for warning to others that may follow the same course hereafter) I have set down the best reckonings that were kept by expert men, William Cox, master of the *Hind*, and John Paul, his mate, both of Limehouse . . . Our course we held in clearing us of these flats was east south-east, and south fourteen leagues with a very scant wind.

The manner how our Admiral ship was lost

Upon Tuesday the twenty-seventh of August, toward the evening, our general caused them in his frigate to sound, who found white sand at thirty-five fathom, being then in latitude about 44 degrees. Wednesday toward night the wind came south, and we bore with the land all that night, west north-west, contrary to the mind of master Cox. Nevertheless we followed the Admiral, deprived of power to prevent a mischief, which by no contradiction could be brought to hold other course, alleging they could not make the ship to work better, nor to lie otherways.

The evening was fair and pleasant, yet not without token of storm to ensue. Most part of this Wednesday night, like the swan that sings before her death, they in the Admiral, of *Delight*, continued in sounding of trumpets, with drum, and fifes; also winding the cornets, oboes; and in the end of their jollity, left with the ringing of doleful knells. Toward the evening also we caught in the *Golden Hind* a very mighty porpoise, with a harpoon. These also passing through the Ocean, in herds, did portend storm. I omit to recite frivolous reports by them in the frigate, of strange voices, the same night, which scared some from the helm.

Thursday the twenty-ninth of August, the wind rose, and blew vehemently at south and by east, bringing rain and thick mist, so that we could not see a cable length before us. And early in the morning we were altogether folded in among flats and sands. We found shoal and deep in every three or four ships' length, after we began to sound. But first we were upon them unawares, until master Cox looking out, discerned (in his judgement) white cliffs, crying 'land'; though we could not afterward descry any land, it being very likely the breaking of the sea white, which seemed to be white cliffs, through the haze and thick weather.

Immediately tokens were given unto the *Delight*, to cast about to seaward, which, being the greater ship, and of burden 120 tons, was yet foremost upon the breach, keeping so ill watch, that they knew not the danger, before they felt the same, too late to recover it. For shortly the Admiral struck aground, and had soon after her stern and hinder parts beaten in pieces. Whereupon the rest (that is to say, the frigate in which was the general and the *Golden Hind*) cast about east south-east, bearing to the south, even for our lives into the wind's eye, because that way carried us to the seaward. At last we recovered (God be thanked) in some despair, to sea room enough.

In this distress, we had vigilant eye unto the Admiral, which we saw cast away, without power to give the men succour. Neither could we espy any of the men that leaped overboard to save themselves, either in the same pinnace or upon rafters, and such like means presenting themselves to men in those extremities; for we desired to save the men by every possible means. But all in vain: all that day, and part of the next, we beat up and down as near unto the wreck as was possible for us, looking out if by good hap we might espy any of them.

This was a heavy and grievous event, to lose at one blow our chief ship freighted with great provision, gathered together with much travail, care, long time, and difficulty. But more was the loss of our men, who perished to the number almost of a hundred souls. Amongst whom was drowned a learned man, an Hungarian, born in the city of Buda, called thereof Budaeus. He of piety and zeal to good attempts, adventured in this action, minding to record in the Latin tongue, the deeds and things worthy of remembrance, happening in this discovery, to the honour of our nation.

Here also perished our German refiner and discoverer of inestimable riches, as it was left among some of us in undoubted hope.

No less heavy was the loss of the captain, Maurice Browne, a virtuous, honest, and discreet gentleman, overseen only in liberty given late before to men that ought to have been restrained. When all hope was past of recovering the ship, and men began to give over and to save themselves, the captain was advised to shift also for his life, by the pinnace at the stern of the ship. But refusing that counsel, he would not give example with the first to leave the ship, but used all means to exhort his people not to despair, nor so to leave off their labour. With this mind he mounted upon the highest deck, where he attended imminent death, and unavoidable: how long, I leave it to God, who withdraws not his comfort from his servants at such times.

In the mean season certain, to the number of fourteen persons, leaped into a small pinnace (the bigness of a Thames barge, which was made in the Newfoundland) cut off the rope wherewith it was towed, and committed themselves to God's mercy, amid the storm and rage of sea and winds, destitute of food, not so much as a drop of fresh water. The boat seeming overcharged in foul weather with company, Edward Headly, a valiant soldier and well reputed of his company, thought better that some of them perished than all, made this motion to cast lots, and them to be thrown overboard upon whom the lots fell, thereby to lighten the boat. He offered himself with the first, content to take his adventure gladly: which nevertheless Richard Clarke, that was master of the Admiral and one of this number, refused, advising to abide God's pleasure, who was able to save all, as well as a few.

The boat was carried before the wind, continuing six days and nights in the Ocean, and arrived at last with the men (alive, but weak) upon the Newfoundland. But Headly, who had been late sick and another called of us Brasil, of his travel into those countries, died by the way, famished. Such was these poor men's extremity, in cold and wet, to have no better sustenance than their own urine, for six days together. Those that arrived upon the Newfoundland, were brought into

France by certain Frenchmen, then being upon that coast.

Our people lost courage daily after this ill fortune, the weather continuing thick and blustering, with increase of cold, winter drawing on, which took from them all hope of amendment. The leeside of us lay full of flats and dangers inevitable, if the wind blew hard at south. Some again suspected we were engulfed in the bay of St Lawrence, the coast full of dangers, and unto us unknown. But above all, provision waxed scant, and hope of supply was gone, with loss of our Admiral.

Those in the frigate were already pinched with spare allowance, and want of clothes chiefly. Whereupon they besought the general to return to England, before they all perished. And to them of the *Golden Hind*, they made signs of their distress, pointing to their mouths, and to their clothes thin and ragged; then immediately they also of the *Golden Hind* grew to be of the same opinion and desire to return home.

The former reasons having also moved the general to have compassion of his poor men, in whom he saw no want of good will, but of means fit to perform the action they came for, resolved upon retire. Calling the captain and master of the *Hind*, he yielded them many reasons enforcing this unexpected return, protesting himself greatly satisfied with that he had seen and knew already. Reiterating these words, 'Be content, we have seen enough, and take no care of expense past: I will set you forth royally the next spring, if God send us safe home. Therefore I pray you let us no longer strive here, where we fight against the elements.' So upon Saturday in the afternoon the thirty-first of August, we changed our course and returned back for England. The wind was large for England at our return, but very high, and the sea rough, insomuch as the frigate wherein the general went was almost swallowed up.

Monday in the afternoon we passed in the sight of Cape Race, having made as much way in little more than two days and nights back again, as before we had done in eight days from Cape Race, unto the place where our ship perished. This hindrance thitherward, and speed back again, are to be imputed unto the swift current, as well as to the winds, which we had more large in our return. This Monday the general came aboard the *Hind* to have the surgeon dress his foot, which he hurt by treading upon a nail. Agreeing to carry our lights always by night that we might keep together, he departed into his frigate, being by no means to be entreated to tarry in the *Hind*, which had been more for his security.

The weather fair, the general came aboard the *Hind* again, to make merry together with the captain, master and company, which was the last meeting, and continued there from morning until night. During which time there passed sundry discourses, touching affairs past and to come; lamenting greatly the loss of his great ship, more of the men, but most of all of his books and notes, and what else I know not, for which he was out of measure grieved. The same doubtless being some matter of more importance than his books, which I could not draw from him. Yet by circumstance I gathered the same to be the ore which Daniel the German had brought unto him in the Newfoundland. Whatsoever it was, the remembrance touched him so deep, as he beat his boy in great rage, even so long after the miscarrying of the great ship, because upon a fair day when we were becalmed upon the coast of the Newfoundland, near unto Cape Race, he sent his boy aboard the Admiral to fetch certain things: amongst which, this being chief was yet forgotten and left behind.

Herein my opinion was better confirmed diversely, and by sundry conjectures which make me have the greater hope of this rich mine. For whereas the general had never before good opinion of these north parts of the world, now his mind was wholly fixed upon the Newfoundland. Also laying down his determination in the spring following, for disposing of his voyage then to be re-attempted, he assigned the captain and master of the *Golden Hind*, unto the south discovery, and reserved unto himself the north; affirming that this voyage had won his heart from the south, and that he was now become a northern man altogether.

Last, being demanded what means he had at his arrival in England to compass the charges of so great preparation as he intended to make the next spring – having determined upon two fleets, one for the south, another for the north: 'Leave that to me,' he replied, 'I will ask a penny of no man. I will bring good tidings unto her Majesty, who will be so gracious to lend me £10,000.' Willing us therefore to be of good cheer; for he did thank God, he said, with all his heart, for that he had seen; the same being enough for us all, and that we needed not to seek any further. And these last words he would often repeat, being himself very confident of inestimable good by this voyage. Which the greater number of his followers nevertheless mistrusted altogether, not being made partakers of those secrets, which the general kept unto himself.

The vehement persuasion and entreaty of his friends could nothing avail to divert him from a wilful resolution of going through in his frigate, which was overcharged upon their decks, with fights, nettings, and small artillery, too cumbersom for so small a boat, that was to pass through the Ocean at that season of the year, when by course we might expect much storm of foul weather, whereof indeed we had enough. But when he was entreated by the captain, master, and others his well-willers of the *Hind* not to venture in the frigate, this was his answer: 'I will not forsake my little company going homeward, with whom I have passed so many storms and perils.' And in very truth, he was urged to be so over-hard, by hard reports given of him that he was afraid of the sea. Albeit this was rather rashness, than advised resolution, to prefer the wind of a vain report to the weight of his own life. Seeing he would not bend to reason, he had provision out of the *Hind*, such as was wanting aboard his frigate. And so we committed him to God's protection, and set him aboard his pinnace, we being more than three hundred leagues onward of our way home.

By that time we had brought the Islands of Azores south of us, yet we then keeping much to the north, until we had got into the height and elevation of England, we met with very foul weather, and terrible seas, breaking short and high pryamid wise. Men which all their life time had occupied the sea never saw more outrageous seas. We had also upon our main yard, an apparition of a little fire by night, which seamen do call Castor and Pollux. But we had only one, which they take an evil sign of more tempest – the same is usual in storms.

Monday the ninth of September, in the afternoon, the frigate was near cast away, oppressed by waves, yet at that time recovered. And giving forth signs of joy, the general sitting abaft with a book in his hand, cried out unto us in the *Hind*, so oft as we did approach within hearing: 'We are as near to heaven by sea as by land.' Reiterating the same speech, well beseeming a soldier, resolute in Jesus Christ, as I can testify he was.

The same Monday night, about twelve of the clock, or not long after, the frigate being ahead of us in the *Golden Hind*, suddenly her lights were out. As it were in a moment we lost the sight, and with that our watch cried, the general was cast away: which was too true. For in that moment, the frigate was devoured and swallowed up by the sea. Yet still we looked out all that night, and even after, until we arrived upon the coast of England; omitting no small sail at sea, unto which we gave not the tokens between us agreed upon, to have perfect knowledge of each other, if we should at any time be separated.

In great torment of weather and peril of drowning, it pleased God to send safe home the *Golden Hind*, which arrived in Falmouth, the twenty-second day of September, being Sunday; not without as great danger escaped in a bluster, coming from the south-east, with such thick mist that we could not discern land, to put in right with the haven.

From Falmouth we went to Dartmouth, and lay there at anchor before the Range, while the captain went on land, to enquire if there had been any news of the frigate, which sailing well, might happily have been before us. Also to certify Sir John Gilbert, brother unto the General, of our hard fortune. He, not altogether despairing of his brother's safety, offered friendship and courtesy to the captain and his company, requiring to have his bark brought into the harbour; in furtherance whereof, a boat was sent to help to tow her in.

Thus have I delivered the contents of the enterprise and last action of Sir Humphrey Gilbert, knight, faithfully, for so much as I thought meet to be published. Herein may always appear, though he be extinguished, some sparks of his virtues, he remaining firm and resolute in a purpose by all pretence honest and godly, as was this, to discover, possess, and to reduce unto the service of God and Christian piety, those remote and heathen countries of America, not actually possessed by Christians, and most rightly appertaining unto the Crown of England. As his zeal deserves high commendation, even so, he may justly be taxed of temerity and presumption (rather) in two respects.

First, when yet there was only probability, not a certain and determinate place of habitation selected, neither any demonstration of commodity there in being, to induce his followers – nevertheless, he both was too prodigal of his own patrimony and too careless of other men's expenses, to employ both his and their substance upon a ground imagined good.

Secondly, when by his former preparation he was enfeebled of ability and credit to perform his designs, as it were impatient to abide in expectation better opportunity and means, he thrust himself again into the action – for which he was not fit, presuming the cause would carry him to the desired end. Having thus made re-entry, he could not yield again to withdraw, though he saw no encouragement to proceed, lest his credit foiled in his first attempt, in a second should utterly be disgraced. Between extremities, he made a right adventure, putting all to God and good fortune and, which was worst, refused not to entertain every person and means whatsoever, to furnish out this expedition, the outcome whereof has been declared.

2

LETTERS FURTHERING WESTERN DISCOVERY

A letter of Sir Francis Walsingham to Mr Richard Hakluyt, then of Christ Church in Oxford, encouraging him in the study of cosmography, and of furthering new discoveries, &c.

I understand as well by a letter I long since received from the Mayor of Bristol, as by conference with Sir George Pekham, that you have endeavoured and given much light for the discovery of the Western parts yet unknown. As your study in these things is very commendable, so I thank you much for the same. Wishing you do continue your travail in these and like matters, which are like to turn not only to your own good in private but to the public benefit of this realm. And so I bid you farewell. From the Court the eleventh of March 1582.

Your loving friend,
Francis Walsingham

A letter of Sir Francis Walsingham to Master Thomas Aldworth, merchant and at that time Mayor of the city of Bristol, concerning their adventure in the Western discovery.

After my hearty commendations, I have for certain causes deferred the answer of your letter of November last till now, which I hope comes all in good time. Your good inclination to the Western discovery I cannot but much commend. And for that Sir Humphrey Gilbert, as you have heard long since, has been preparing into those parts, being ready to embark within these ten days, who needs some further supply of shipping than yet he has, I am of opinion that you shall do well if the ship or two barks you write of be put in a readiness to go along with him, or so soon after as you may. I hope this travail will prove profitable to the Adventurers and generally beneficial to the whole realm. Herein I pray you confer with these bearers, Mr Richard Hakluyt, and Mr Thomas Steventon, to whom I refer you. And so bid you heartily farewell. Richmond the eleventh of March 1582.

Your loving friend,
Francis Walsingham

A letter written from Mr Thomas Aldworth, merchant and mayor of the city of Bristol, to the right honourable Sir Francis Walsingham, principal Secretary to her Majesty, concerning a Western voyage intended for the discovery of the coast of America, lying to the south-west of Cape Breton.

Right honourable, upon the receipt of your letters directed unto me and delivered by the bearers hereof, Mr Richard Hakluyt and Mr Steventon, bearing date the eleventh of March, I presently conferred with my friends in private, whom I know most affectionate to this enterprise, especially with Mr William Saltern deputy of our company of merchants. Whereupon, myself being as then sick, with as convenient speed as he could, he caused an assembly of the merchants to be gathered. After dutiful mention of your honourable disposition for the benefit of this city, he by my appointment caused your letters to be read in public, and after some good light given by Mr Hakluyt unto them that were ignorant of the country and enterprise and were desirous to be resolved, the motion grew generally so well to be liked, that there was set down by men's own hands then present and very willing offer, the sum of 1000 marks and upward [£666 13s 4d]. If it should not suffice, we doubt not but otherwise to furnish out for this Western discovery a ship of three-score and a bark of 40 tons, to be left in the country under the direction and government of your son-in-law Mr Carlile, of whom we have heard much good, if it shall stand with your honour's good liking and his acceptation. In one of which barks we are also willing to have Mr Steventon, your honour's messenger and one well known to us, as captains. And here in humble manner, desiring your honour to vouchsafe us of your further direction by a general letter to myself, my brethren, and the rest of the merchants of this city, at your honour's best and most convenient leisure, because we mean not to defer the final proceeding in this voyage, any further than to the end of April next coming, I cease, beseeching God long to bless and prosper your honourable estate. Bristol. March twenty-seventh 1583.

A letter sent to the right Honourable Sir William Cecil, Lord Burghley, Lord High Treasurer of England &c. From Mr Thomas James of Bristol, concerning the discovery of Magdalen Isle, dated the fourteenth of September 1591.

Right Honourable, my humble duty to your good lordship done, I thought good humbly to advertise your honour of the discovery of an island made by two small ships of Saint Malo; the one eight days past being prized near Scilly by a ship of which I am part owner, called the *Pleasure*, sent by this city to my Lord Thomas Howard, for her Majesty's service. Which prize is sent back to this port by those of the said ships, with upwards of forty tons of train-oil. The island lies in 47 degrees some fifty leagues from the Grand Bay, near Newfoundland; and is about twenty leagues about, and some part of the island is flat sands and shoal. The fish come on the banks (to do their kind) in April, May and June, by numbers of thousands. Which fish is very big, and has two great teeth; the skin of them is like buff's leather; and they will not away from their young ones. The young ones are as good meat as veal. With the bellies of five of the said fish they make a hogshead of train-oil, which is very sweet and, if it will make soap, the king of Spain may burn some of his olive trees. Humbly praying your lordship to pardon herein my boldness, betaking your honour to the keeping of the Almighty. From Bristol, this fourteenth of September 1591.

Your honour's most humbly at commandment,

Thomas James

A Brief Note of the Walrus

In the first voyage of Jaques Cartier, wherein he discovered the gulf of St Lawrence and the said Isle of Magdalen in the year 1534, he met with these beasts, as he witnesses in these words. About the said island are very great beasts as great as oxen, which have two great teeth in their mouths like unto elephants' teeth, and live in the sea. We saw one of them sleeping upon the bank of the water and, thinking to take it, we went to it with our boats, but so soon as he heard us he cast himself into the sea. They are called in Latin *Boves Marini*, or *Vaccae Marinae*, and in the Russian tongue *Morsses*; their hides I have seen as big as any ox-hide and, being dressed, I have yet a piece of one thicker than any two ox or bull's hides in England. The leather-dressers take them to be excellent good to make light shields against the arrows of the savages. I hold them far better than the light leather shields which the Moors use in Barbary against arrows and lances, where I have seen divers in her Majesty's stately Armoury in the Tower of London.

The teeth of the said fishes, whereof I have seen a basketful at once, are a foot and sometimes more in length. They have been sold in England to the comb and knife-makers at 8 groats and 3 shillings the pound weight; whereas the best ivory is sold for half the money. The grain of the bone is somewhat more yellow than the ivory. One Mr Alexander Woodson of Bristol, my old friend, an excellent mathematician and skilful physician, showed me one of these beasts' teeth which were brought from the Isle of Magdalen in the first prize, which was half a yard long or very little less, and assured me that he had made trial of it in ministering medicine to his patients, and had found it as sovereign against poison as any unicorn's horn.

3

THE *MARIGOLD*'S VOYAGE TO
NEWFOUNDLAND, 1593

The voyage of the ship called the Marigold *of Mr Hill of Rotherhithe
unto Cape Breton and beyond to the latitude of 44 degrees and a half, 1593.
Written by Richard Fisher, master Hill's man of Rotherhithe.*

The ship called the *Marigold* of 70 tons in burden furnished
with twenty men, whereof ten were mariners, the master's
name being Richard Strong of Topsham, the master's mate
Peter Langworth of Topsham, with three coopers, two
butchers to flay the walruses (whereof divers have teeth above
a cubit long and skins far thicker than any bull's hide) with
other necessary people, departed out of Falmouth the first of
June 1593. In consort with another ship of Mr Drake's of
Topsham, which upon some occasion was not ready so soon
as she should have been by two months.

The place for which these two ships were bound was an
island within the straits of Saint Peter on the back side of
Newfoundland to the south-west, in the latitude of 47 degrees, called by the Bretons of Saint Malo the isle of Ramea,
but by the savages and naturals of the continent next adjoining, Menquit. On which isle are so great abundance of the
huge and mighty walruses with great teeth in the months of
April, May and June that there have been fifteen hundred
killed there by one small bark, in the year 1591. The two
English ships aforesaid lost company before they came to
Newfoundland, and never came after together in all their
voyage. The ship of Mr George Drake fell first with New-

foundland, and afterward directly came to the isle of Ramea, though too late in the year to make her voyage.

Here our men took certain walruses, but not in such numbers as they might have had, if they had come in due season, which they had neglected. The *Marigold* fell with Cape St Francis in Newfoundland the eleventh of July; thence we went into the bay Rogneuse, and afterward doubled Cape Ray. Sailing toward the strait of Saint Peter (which is the entrance between Newfoundland and Cape Breton), being unacquainted with the place, beat up and down a very long time, and yet missed it. We at length overshot it, and fell with Cape Breton.

Here divers of our men went on land upon the very cape, where they found the spits of oak of the savages who had roasted meat a little before. They saw divers beasts and fowls, as black foxes, deer, otters, great fowls with red legs, penguins, and certain others. But having found no people here at this our first landing we went again on shipboard, and sailed farther four leagues to the west of Cape Breton, where we saw many seals. Having need of fresh water we went again on shore; and passing somewhat more into the land, we found certain round ponds artificially made by the savages to keep fish in, with weirs in them made to take fish.

We had not been long here but there came one savage, with black long hair hanging about his shoulders, who called unto us, weaving his hands downward towards his belly, using these words, 'Calitogh, Calitogh'. As we drew towards him one of our men's musket unawares shot off; whereupon he fell down, and rising up suddenly again, he cried thrice with a loud voice 'Chiogh, Chiogh, Chiogh'. Thereupon nine or ten of his fellows running right up over the bushes with great agility and swiftness came towards us, with white staves in their hands like half pikes. Their dogs of colour black, not so big as a greyhound, followed them at the heels. But we retired unto our boat without any hurt at all. Howbeit one of them broke an hogshead which we had filled with fresh water, with a great branch of a tree which lay on the ground. Upon which occasion we bestowed half a dozen musket-shot upon them, which they avoided by falling flat to the earth, and afterward retired to the woods.

One of the savages, who seemed to be their captain, wore a long mantle of beasts' skins hanging on one of his shoulders. The rest were all naked except their privities, which were covered with a skin tied behind. After they had escaped our shot they made a great fire on the shore, belike to give their fellows warning of us.

The kinds of trees that we noted were goodly oaks, fir trees of a great height, a kind of tree called of us quickbeam, and cherry trees, and divers other kinds to us unknown, because we stayed not long with diligence to observe them. There is great show of resin, pitch, and tar. We found in both the places where we went abundance of raspberries, strawberries, hurts, and herbs of good smell, and divers good for the scurvy, and grass very rank and of great length. We saw five or six boats sailing to the south-westwards of Cape Breton, which we judged to be Christians, which had some trade that way. We saw also the manner of their hanging up their fish and flesh with withies to dry in the air. They also lay them upon rafts and hurdles and make a smoke under them, or a soft fire, and so dry them as the savages do in Virginia.

While we lay four leagues south of Cape Breton we sounded and had sixty fathoms black oozy ground. Sailing thence westward nine or ten leagues off the shore, we had twenty-four fathoms red sand, and small whitish stones. We continued our course so far to the south-west that we brought ourselves into the latitude of 44 degrees and a half, having sailed fifty or sixty leagues to the south-west of Cape Breton. We found the current between Cape Breton and Cape Ray to set out toward the east south-east. In our course to the west of Cape Breton we saw exceeding great store of seals, and abundance of porpoises, whereof we killed eleven. We saw whales also of all sorts as well small as great. Here our men took many bearded cod with one teat underneath, which are like to the north-east cods, and better than those of Newfoundland.

From our arrival at the haven of Saint Francis in Newfoundland, we continued beating up and down to the west and south-west of Cape Breton until the twenty-eighth of September. Then we shaped our course homeward by the isles of the Azores, and came first to Corvo and Flores, where beating up and down and missing of expected prey, having wasted all our victuals, we were constrained against our wills to hasten home unto our Narrow Seas.

One thing very strange happened in this voyage. A mighty great whale followed our ship for many days as we passed by Cape Race, which by no means we could chase from our ship. Until one of our men fell overboard and was drowned; after which she immediately forsook us, and never afterward appeared unto us.

4

THE NEWFOUNDLAND VOYAGE OF THE *GRACE*, 1594

The voyage of the Grace *of Bristol of Mr Rice Jones, a bark of 35 tons, up into the bay of Saint Lawrence to the north-west of Newfoundland, as far as the isle of Assumption or Anticosti, for the fins of whales and train-oil. Made by Silvester Wyet, shipmaster, of Bristol.*

We departed with the aforesaid bark manned with twelve men for the place aforesaid from Bristol the fourth of April 1594, and fell with Cape d'Espoir on the coast of Newfoundland the nineteenth of May in the height of 47. We went thence for Cape Race, being distant from thence eighteen or nineteen leagues, the very same day. The twentieth day we were thwart of Cape Race. Then we set our course north-west for Cape St Mary, which is distant from Cape Race nineteen leagues, and is on the ease side of the great Bay of Placentia almost at the entry thereof.

From thence we shaped our course for the islands of St Pierre, passing by the broken islands of the Martyrs. In these isles of St Pierre there is a fair harbour, which we went into with our bark, and found there two ships of Sibiburo fishing for cod. Here we stayed two days, and took in ballast for our ship. There are as fair and tall fir trees growing therein as in any other part of Newfoundland. As we came out of the harbour's mouth we laid the ship upon the lee, and in two hours' space we took with our hooks three or four hundred great cods for provision of our ship. Then we departed from the isle of St Pierre to enter into the gulf of St Lawrence between Cape Breton and the said isle, and set our course west north-west, and fell with Cape Ray. From Cape Ray to Cape Anguille we set our course north north-west, thence into the bay of St George.

In this bay we found the wrecks of two great Biscayan ships, which had been cast away three years before. Where we found some seven or eight hundred whale fins, and some iron bolts and chains of their main shrouds and fore shrouds. All their train-oil was beaten out with the weather, but the cask remained still. Some part of the commodities were spoiled by tumbling down of the cliffs, which covered part of the cask, and the greater part of those whale fins, which we understood to be there by four Spaniards who escaped and were brought to St Jean de Luz.

Here we found the houses of the savages, made of fir trees bound together in the top and set round like a dovehouse, and covered with the barks of fir trees. We found also some part of their victuals, deers' flesh roasted upon wooden spits at the fire, and a dish made of bark of a tree, sowed together with the sinews of the deer, wherein was oil of the deer. There were also cormorants, which they had plucked and made ready to have dressed, and we found a wooden spoon of their making. We discerned the tracks of some forty or fifty men, women and children.

Being informed that the whales which are deadly wounded in the Grand Bay, and yet escape the fisher, are wont to shoot themselves on shore on the isle of Anticosti, which lies in the very mouth of the great river that runs up to Canada, we shaped our course over to that long isle and found the distance to the easternmost end to be about forty-four leagues. Here we arrived about the midst of June at the east end, and rode in eighteen fathom water in fair white sand and very good anchorage, and for trial heaved a line overboard and found wonderful great cod fish. From the eastern end we went to the northern side of the island, which we perceived to be but narrow in respect of the length thereof. After we had searched two days and a night for the whales which we hoped to have found there, and missed of our purpose, we returned back to the southward, and were within one league of the island of Penguin.

Thence returned we by the isles of St Pierre, and so came

into the bay of Placentia. We arrived in the eastern side thereof among the fishermen of St Jean de Luz and of Biscay. They were to the number of threescore and odd sails, whereof eight ships only were Spaniards, of whom we were very well used, and they wished heartily for peace between them and us. There the men of St Jean bestowed two pinnaces on us to make up our voyage with fish.

Then we departed over to the other side of the bay, where we arrived in an harbour which is called Pesmarck. There we made our stage and fished so long that in the end the savages came, and in the night cut both our pinnace and our ship's boat away to our great hindrance. Yet it was our good fortune to find out our pinnaces and get them again. For fear of a shrewder turn of the savages we departed for Cape St Mary, and having passed Cape Race, we arrived in Farrillon. Finding there two-and-twenty sails of Englishmen, we made up our fishing voyage to the full in that harbour, the twenty-fourth of August, to our good content. Departing thence we arrived in the river of Bristol, by the grace of God, the twenty-fourth of September 1594.

5

LEIGH'S REPORT OF NEWFOUNDLAND AND THE APPROACHES TO CANADA, 1597

Newfoundland we found very subject to fogs and mists. The ground of it is very rocky; upon it there is great store of fir trees, and in some places red; about the shore it has great abundance of cod-fish. We were on land in it in four several places: 1. At Caplin bay and Farrillon; 2. At Cape Race; 3. At the harbour of Lano, which lies four leagues to the west beyond Cape Lawrence; 4. At St Mary port.

The island of Menego for the soil is much like Newfoundland, but the fish about it, as also throughout the Grand Bay within Cape Breton, is much larger and better than that of Newfoundland. This island is scant two leagues long, and very narrow. In the midst of it, a great way within the wood, is a great pool. Here we were thrice on shore; once at the east side, and twice at the west.

The three islands of Birds are sandy red, but with the multitude of birds upon them they look white. The birds sit there as thick as stones lie in a paved street. The greatest of the islands is about a mile in compass. The second is a little less. The third is a very little one, like a small rock. At the second of these three lay on the shore in the sunshine about thirty or forty walruses which, when our boat came near them, presently made into the sea, and swam after the boat.

Brion's Island we found to be very good, and sandy ground. It has in it store of fir trees. It is somewhat more than a league long, and about three leagues in compass. Here we were on land once, and went from the one side of it to the other.

The island of Ramea we took to be like ground as Brion's Island, having also abundance of fir trees. It seems to be in length about twelve or thirteen leagues at least. We were there in harbour, but not on shore, which we much desired and hoped to have been; but the conflict which we had there with the Basques and Bretons prevented us.

The Isle Blanche likewise seems in quality of the ground and bigness of it to be much like Brion's Island aforesaid, but somewhat less. We were not on shore upon it, but rode before it at anchor.

The land of Cape Breton we found to be somewhat like Newfoundland, but rather better. Here toward the west end of it we saw the clouds lie lower than the hills; as we did also at Cape Lawrence in Newfoundland. The easterly end of the land of Cape Breton is nothing so high land as the west. We went on shore upon it in five places: 1. At the bay where the *Chancewell* was cast away; 2. At Cibo; 3. At a little island between Cibo and the New Port; 4. At the New Port; And 5. At Port Ingles, or the English Port.

Concerning the nature and fruitfulness of Brion's Island, Isle Blanche, and of Ramea, they do by nature yield exceeding plenty of wood, great store of wild corn like barley, strawberries, gooseberries, mulberries, white roses, and store of wild peas. Also about the said islands the sea yields great abundance of fish of divers sorts; and they also seem to proffer, through the labour of man, plenty of all kind of our grain, of roots, of hemp, and other necessary commodities.

6

SIR WALTER RALEIGH'S LETTERS PATENT FOR VIRGINIA, 1584

The Voyages and Navigations of the English nation to Virginia, and the several discoveries thereof, chiefly at the charges of the honourable Sir Walter Raleigh, knight, from 33 to 30 degrees of latitude. Together with the success of the English colonies there planted; as likewise a description of the Country, with the Inhabitants, and the manifold commodities.

The letters patents, granted by the Queen's Majesty to Mr Walter Raleigh, now knight, for the discovering and planting of new lands and countries, to continue the space of six years and no more.

Elizabeth by the grace of God of England, France and Ireland Queen, defender of the faith, &c. To all people to whom these presents shall come, greeting. Know ye that of our especial grace, certain science, and mere motion, we have given and granted to our trusty and wellbeloved servant, Walter Raleigh Esquire, free liberty and licence from time to time to discover, search, find out, and view such remote, heathen and barbarous lands, countries, and territories, not actually possessed by any Christian prince, nor inhabited by Christian people. The same to have, hold, occupy and enjoy to him, his heirs and assigns for ever, with all prerogatives, commodites, jurisdictions, royalties, privileges, franchises and pre-eminences thereto or thereabouts both by sea and land, whatsoever we by our letters patents may grant . . . All which lands, countries, and territories shall for ever be held by the said Walter Raleigh, his heirs and assigns, for us, our heirs and successors, by homage, and by the payment of the fifth part, reserved only for all services . . .

. . . Provided always, and our will and pleasure is, and we do hereby declare to all Christian kings, princes, and states, that if the said Walter Raleigh, his heirs of assigns, or any other by their licence or appointment shall at any time hereafter rob or spoil by sea or by land, or do any act of unjust or unlawful hostility, to any of the subjects of us, our heirs or successors, or to any of the subjects of any the kings, princes, rulers, governors, or estates in perfect league and amity with us, we shall make open Proclamation that the said Walter Raleigh, his heirs and assigns and adherents shall make full restitution and satisfaction of all such injuries done.

Witness ourselves, at Westminster the five-and-twentieth day of March, in the six-and-twentieth year of our reign [1584].

7

THE FIRST VIRGINIA VOYAGE, 1584

The first voyage made to the coasts of America, with two barks, wherein were captains Philip Amadas, and Arthur Barlow, who discovered part of the country now called Virginia, anno 1584. Written by one of the said captains, and sent to Sir Walter Raleigh, knight, at whose charge and direction, the said voyage was set forth.

The twenty-seventh day of April, in the year of our redemption 1584, we departed the west of England, with two barks well furnished with men and victuals, having received our last and perfect directions by your letters, confirming the former instructions, and commandments delivered by yourself at our leaving the river Thames. And I think it a matter both unnecessary, for the manifest discovery of the country, as also for tediousness sake, to remember unto you the diurnal of our course, sailing thither and returning. Only I have presumed to present unto you this brief discourse, by which you may judge how profitable this land is likely to succeed, as well to yourself, by whose direction and charge, and by whose servants this our discovery has been performed, as also to her Highness, and the common wealth. We hope your wisdom will be satisfied, considering that as much by us has been brought to light, as by those small means and number of men we had, could any way have been expected, or hoped for.

The tenth of May we arrived at the Canaries, and the tenth of June we were fallen with the islands of the West Indies, keeping a more south-easterly course than was needful. Because we doubted that the current of the Bay of Mexico, flowing between the Cape of Florida and Havana, had been of greater force than afterwards we found it to be. At which islands we found the air very unwholesome, and our men grew for the most part ill disposed. So that having refreshed ourselves with sweet water and fresh victual, we departed the twelfth day of our arrival there. These islands, with the rest adjoining, are so well known to yourself and to many others, as I will not trouble you with the remembrance of them.

The second of July, we found shoal water, where we smelt so sweet and so strong a smell, as if we had been in the midst of some delicate garden abounding with all kind of odoriferous flowers. By which we were assured that the land could not be far distant. Keeping good watch and bearing but slack sail, the fourth of the same month we arrived upon the coast, which we supposed to be a continent and firm land. We sailed along the same a hundred and twenty English miles before we could find any entrance, or river issuing into the sea. The first that appeared unto us we entered, though not without some difficulty, and cast anchor about three harquebus-shot within the haven's mouth, on the left hand of the same.

After thanks given to God for our safe arrival thither, we manned our boats, and went to view the land next adjoining, and 'to take possession of the same, in the right of the Queen's most excellent Majesty, as rightful Queen of the same'. And after we delivered the same over to your use, according to her Majesty's grant and letters patents, under her Highness' great seal.

This being performed, according to the ceremonies used in such enterprises, we viewed the land about us, being, where we first landed, very sandy and low towards the water's side; but so full of grapes as the very beating and surge of the sea overflowed them. We found such plenty as well there as in all places else, both on the sand and on the green soil on the hills, as in the plains, as well on every little shrub, as also climbing towards the tops of high cedars, that I think in all the world the like abundance is not to be found.

We passed from the seaside towards the tops of those hills next adjoining, being but of mean height, and from thence we beheld the sea on both sides to the north and to the south, finding no end any of both ways. This land lay stretching itself to the west, which after we found to be but an island of twenty miles long, and not above six miles broad. Under the bank or hill whereon we stood, we beheld the valleys replenished with goodly cedar trees. Having discharged our harquebus-shot, such a flock of cranes (the most part white) arose under us, with such a cry redoubled by many echoes, as if an army of men had shouted all together.

This island had many goodly woods full of deer, conies, hares, and fowl, even in the midst of summer in incredible abundance. The woods are not such as you find on Bohemia, Moscovy, or Siberia, barren and fruitless, but the highest and reddest cedars of the world, far bettering the cedars of the Azores, of the Indies, or Lebanon; pine, cypress, sassafras, the lentisk, or the tree that bears the mastic; the tree that bears the rind of black cinnamon, of which master Winter brought from the straits of Magellan, and many other of excellent smell and quality.

We remained by the side of this island two whole days before we saw any people of the country. The third day we spied one small boat rowing towards us, having in it three persons. This boat came to the island side, four harquebus-shot from our ships; there two of the people remaining, the third came along the shoreside towards us. We being then all within board, he walked up and down upon the point of the land next unto us. Then the master and the pilot of the Admiral, Simon Ferdinandez, and the captain Philip Amadas, myself, and others rowed to the land, whose coming this fellow attended, never making any show of fear or doubt. And after he had spoken of many things not understood by us, we brought him with his own good liking aboard the ships, and gave him a shirt, a hat and some other things, and made him taste of our wine and our meat, which he liked very well. After having viewed both barks he departed, and went to his own boat again, which he had left in a little cove or creek adjoining. As soon as he was two bow shot into the water, he fell to fishing; and in less than half an hour, he had laden his boat as deep as it could swim, with which he came again to the point of the land. There he divided his fish into two parts, pointing one part to the ship, and the other to the pinnace. After he had (as much as he might) requited the former benefits received, he departed out of our sight.

The next day there came unto us divers boats, and in one of them the king's brother, accompanied with forty or fifty men, very handsome and goodly people, and in their behaviour as mannerly and civil as any of Europe. His name was Granganimeo, and the king is called Wingina, the country Wingandacoa, and now by her Majesty Virginia. The manner of his coming was in this sort: he left his boats altogether as the first man did a little from the ships by the shore, and came along to the place over against the ships, followed with forty men. When he came to the place, his servants spread a long mat upon the ground, on which he sat down; at the other end of the mat four others of his company did the like; the rest of his men stood round about him, somewhat afar off. When we came to the shore to him with our weapons, he never moved from his place, nor any of the other four; nor ever mistrusted any harm to be offered from us, but sitting still he beckoned us to come and sit by him, which we performed. Being set he made all signs of joy and welcome, striking on his head and his breast and afterwards on ours, to show we were all one, smiling and making show the best he could of all love and familiarity. After he had made a long speech unto us, we presented him with divers things, which he received very joyfully and thankfully. None of the company durst speak one word all the time; only the four which were at the other end spoke one in the other's ear very softly.

The king is greatly obeyed, and his brothers and children reverenced. The king himself in person was at our being there, sore wounded in a fight which he had with the king of the next country, called Wingina, and was shot in two places through the body, and once clean through the thigh, but yet he recovered. By reason whereof and for that he lay at the chief town of the country, being six days journey off, we saw him not at all.

After we had presented his brother with such things as we thought he liked, we likewise gave somewhat to the other that sat with him on the mat. But at once he arose and took all from them, and put it into his own basket, making signs and tokens that all things ought to be delivered unto him, and the rest were but his servants, and followers. A day or two after this, we fell to trading with them, exchanging some things that we had for chamois, buff, and deer skins. When we showed him all our packet of merchandise, of all things that he saw a bright tin dish most pleased him. This he immediately took up and clapped it before his breast, and after made a hole in the brim thereof and hung it about his neck, making signs that it would defend him against his enemies' arrows. For those people maintain a deadly and terrible war with the people and king adjoining. We exchanged our tin dish for twenty skins, worth twenty crowns or twenty nobles; and a copper kettle for fifty skins worth fifty crowns. They offered us good exchange for our hatchets and axes, and for knives, and would have given anything for swords; but we would not part with any.

After two or three days the king's brother came aboard the ships and drank wine, and ate of our meat and of our bread, and liked exceedingly thereof. After a few days overpassed, he brought his wife with him to the ships, his daughter and two or three children. His wife was very well favoured, of mean stature, and very bashful. She had on her back a long cloak of leather, with the fur side next to her body, and before her a piece of the same; about her forehead she had a band of white coral, and so had her husband many times. In her ears she had bracelets of pearls hanging down to her middle (whereof we delivered your worship a little bracelet), and those were of the bigness of good peas. The rest of her women of the better sort had pendants of copper hanging in either ear, and some of the children of the king's brother and other noble men have five or six in either ear. He himself had upon his head a broad plate of gold or copper, for being unpolished we knew not what metal it should be; neither would he by any means suffer us to take it off his head, but feeling it, it would bow very easily. His apparel was as his wives', only the women wear their hair long on both sides, and the men but on one. They are of colour yellowish, and their hair black for the most part, and yet we saw children that had very fine auburn and chestnut coloured hair.

After that these women had been there, there came down

from all parts great store of people, bringing with them leather, coral, divers kinds of dyes very excellent, and exchanged with us. But when Granganimeo the king's brother was present, none durst trade but himself, except such as wear red pieces of copper on their heads like himself. For that is the difference between the noblemen and governors of countries, and the meaner sort. We both noted there, and you have understood since by these men which we brought home, that no people in the world carry more respect to their king, nobility, and governors than these do. The king's brother's wife, when she came to us (as she did many times) was followed with forty or fifty women always. When she came into the ship, she left them all on land, saving her two daughters, her nurse and one or two more. The king's brother always kept his order: as many boats as he would come with to the ships, so many fires would he make on the shore afar off, to the end we might understand with what strength and company he approached.

Their boats are made of one tree, either of pine or of pitch trees: a wood not commonly known to our people, nor found growing in England. They have no edge-tools to make them with: if they have any they are very few, and those it seems they had twenty years since. This, as those two men declared, was out of a wreck which happened upon their coast of some Christian ship, being beaten that way by some storm and outrageous weather. None of the people were saved, but only the ship, or some part of her being cast upon the sand, out of whose sides they drew the nails and the spikes, and with those they made their best instruments. The manner of making their boats is thus: they burn down some great tree, or take such as are wind-fallen, and putting gum and resin upon one side thereof, they set fire into it. When it has burnt it hollow, they cut out the coal with their shells, and ever where they would burn it deeper or wider they lay on gums, which burn away the timber. By this means they fashion very fine boats, and such as will transport twenty men. Their oars are like scoops, and many times they set with long poles, as the depth serves.

The king's brother had great liking for our armour, a sword, and divers other things which we had, and offered to lay a great box of pearl in gage for them. But we refused it for this time, because we would not make them know that we esteemed thereof, until we had understood in what places of the country the pearl grew: which now your worship does very well understand.

He was very just of his promise; for many times we delivered him merchandise upon his word, but ever he came within the day and performed his promise. He sent us every day a brace or two of fat bucks, conies, hares, fish the best of the world. He sent us divers kinds of fruits, melons, walnuts, cucumbers, gourds, peas, and divers roots, and fruits very excellent good. And of their country corn, which is very white, fair and well tasted, and grows three times in five months. In May they sow, in July they reap, in June they sow, in August they reap; in July they sow, in September they reap. Only they cast the corn into the ground, breaking a little of the soft turf with a wooden mattock, or pickaxe. Ourselves proved the soil, and put some of our peas in the ground, and in ten days they were of fourteen inches high. They have also beans very fair of divers colours and wonderful plenty; some growing naturally, and some in their gardens, and so have they both wheat and oats.

The soil is most plentiful, sweet, fruitful and wholesome of all the world. There are above fourteen several sweet-smelling timber trees, and the most part of their underwoods are bays and such like. They have those oaks that we have, but far greater and better.

After they had been divers times aboard our ships, myself with seven more went twenty mile into the river that runs toward the city of Skicoak, which river they call Occam. The evening following we came to an island, which they call Roanoke, distant from the harbour by which we entered seven leagues. At the north end thereof was a village of nine houses, built of cedar, and fortified round about with sharp trees, to keep out their enemies, and the entrance into it made like a turnpike very skilfully. When we came towards it, standing near unto the water's side, the wife of Granganimeo the king's brother came running out to meet us very cheerfully and friendly. Her husband was not then in the village; some of her people she commanded to draw our boat on shore for the beating of the billow; others she appointed to carry us on their backs to the dry ground, and others to bring our oars into the house for fear of stealing. When we were come into the outer room, having five rooms in her house, she caused us to sit down by a great fire, and after took off our clothes and washed them, and dried them again. Some of the women plucked off our stockings and washed them, some washed our feet in warm water. She herself took great pains to see all things ordered in the best manner she could, making great haste to dress some meat for us to eat.

After we had thus dried ourselves, she brought us into the inner room, where she set on the board standing along the house, some wheat like frumenty, sodden venison and roasted, fish sodden, boiled, and roasted; melons raw and sodden, roots of divers kinds, and divers fruits. Their drink is commonly water, but while the grape lasts they drink wine; for want of casks to keep it, all the year after they drink water. But it is sodden with ginger in it, and black cinnamon, and sometimes sassafras, and divers other wholesome and medicinable herbs. We were entertained with all love and kindness, and with as much bounty (after their manner) as they could possibly devise. We found the people most gentle, loving, and faithful, void of all guile and treason, and such as live after the manner of the golden age. The people only care how to defend themselves from the cold in their short winter, and to feed themselves with such meat as the soil affords. Their meat is very well sodden and they make broth very sweet and savoury. Their vessels are earthen pots, very large, white and sweet, their dishes are wooden platters of sweet timber. Within the place where they feed was their lodging, and within that their idol, which they worship, of whom they speak incredible things.

While we were at meat, there came in at the gates two or three men with their bows and arrows from hunting, whom when we spied, we began to look one towards another, and offered to reach our weapons. But as soon as she spied our mistrust, she was very much moved, and caused some of her men to run out, and take away their bows and arrows and break them, and beat the poor fellows out of the gate again. When we departed in the evening and would not tarry all night, she was very sorry, and gave us into our boat our supper half-dressed, pots and all, and brought us to our boat side. In which we lay all night, removing the same a pretty distance from the shore. She, perceiving our distrust, was much grieved, and sent divers men and thirty women to sit all night on the bank side by us. She sent us into our boats five mats to cover us from the rain, using very many words to entreat us to rest in their houses. But because we were few men, and if we had miscarried, the voyage had been in very great danger, we durst not adventure anything, though there was no cause for doubt. For a more kind and loving people there can not be found in the world, as far as we have hitherto had trial.

Beyond this island there is the mainland, and over against this island falls into this spacious water, the great river called Occam by the inhabitants. On this stands a town called Pomeiock; six days' journey from the same is situate their greatest city, called Skicoak, which this people affirm to be very great. But the savages were never at it; only they speak of it by the report of their fathers and other men, whom they have heard affirm it to be above one hour's journey about.

Into this river falls another great river, called Cipo, in which there is found great store of mussels in which there are pearls. Likewise there descends into this Occam another river, called Nomapana. On the one side stands a great town called Chawanook, and the lord of that town and country is called Pooneno. This Pooneno is not subject to the king of Wingandacoa, but is a free lord. Beyond this country is there another king, whom they call Menatonon. These three kings are in league with each other. Towards the southwest, four days' journey is situate a town called Secotan, which is the southernmost town of Wingandacoa. Near this, six-and-twenty years past, there was a ship cast away, whereof some of the people were saved, and those were white people, whom the country people preserved.

And after ten days remaining in an out island uninhabited, called Wocokon, they with the help of some of the dwellers of Secotan, fastened two boats of the country together and made masts unto them and sails of their shirts. Having taken into them such victuals as the country yielded, they departed after they had remained in this out island three weeks. But shortly after it seemed they were cast away, for the boats were found upon the coast, cast on land in another island adjoining. Other than these, there was never any people apparelled, or white of colour, either seen or heard of amongst these people, and these aforesaid were seen only of the inhabitants of Secotan. This appeared to be very true, for they wondered marvellously when we were amongst them at the whiteness of our skins, even coveting to touch our breasts, and view the same.

Besides they had our ships in marvellous admiration, and all things else were so strange unto them as it appeared that none of them had ever seen the like. When we discharged any piece, were it but an harquebus, they would tremble thereat for very fear, and for the strangeness of the same. For the weapons which themselves use are bows and arrows: the arrows are but of small canes, headed with a sharp shell or tooth of a fish sufficient enough to kill a naked man. Their swords be of wood hardened; likewise they use wooden breastplates for their defence. They have besides a kind of club, in the end whereof they fasten the sharp horns of a stag, or other beast. When they go to wars they carry about with them their idol, of whom they ask counsel, as the Romans were wont of the Oracle of Apollo. They sing songs as they march towards battle instead of drums and trumpets. Their wars are very cruel and bloody, by reason whereof, and of their civil dissensions which have happened of late years amongst them, the people are marvellously wasted, and in some places the country left desolate.

Adjoining to this country aforesaid called Secotan begins a country called Pomovik, belonging to another king whom they call Piemacum. This king is in league with the next king adjoining towards the setting of the sun, and the country Newsiok, situate upon a goodly river called Neus. These kings have mortal war with Wingina, king of Wingandacoa. But about two years past there was a peace made between the king Piemacum, and the lord of Secotan, as these men which we have brought with us to England have given us to understand. But there remains a mortal malice in the Secotans for many injuries and slaughters done upon them by this

Piemacum. They invited divers men and thirty women of the best of his country to their town to a feast. When they were altogether merry, and praying before their idol (which is nothing else but a mere illusion of the devil), the captain or lord of the town came suddenly upon them, and slew them every one, reserving the women and children. These two have oftentimes since persuaded us to surprise Piemacum's town, having promised and assured us, that there will be found in it great store of commodities. But whether their persuasion be to the end they may be revenged of their enemies, or for the love they bear to us, we leave that to the trial hereafter.

Beyond this island called Roanoke are main islands very plentiful of fruits and other natural increases, together with many towns and villages, along the side of the continent, some bounding upon the islands, and some stretching up further into the land.

When we first had sight of this country, some thought the first land we saw to be the continent. But after we entered into the haven, we saw before us another mightly long sea. For there lies along the coast a tract of islands, two hundred miles in length, adjoining to the Ocean, and between the islands, two or three entrances. When you are entered between them (these islands being very narrow for the most part, as in most places six miles broad, in some places less, in few more), then there appears another great sea, containing in breadth in some places, forty, and in some fifty, in some twenty miles over, before you come unto the continent. In this enclosed sea there are above an hundred islands of divers bignesses. One is sixteen miles long, at which we were, finding it a most pleasant and fertile ground, replenished with goodly cedars, and divers other sweet woods, full of currants, of flax, and many other notable commodities, which we at that time had no leisure to view. Besides this island there are many, some of two, or three, of four, of five miles, some more, some less, most beautiful and pleasant to behold, replenished with deer, conies, hares and divers beasts, and about them the goodliest and best fish in the world, and in great abundance.

Thus sir, we have acquainted you with the particulars of

our discovery, made this present voyage, as far forth as the shortness of the time we there continued would afford us take view of. So contenting ourselves with this service at this time, which we hope hereafter to enlarge, as occasion and assistance shall be given, we resolved to leave the country, and to apply ourselves to return to England. This we did accordingly, and arrived safely in the west of England about the midst of September.

And whereas we have above certified you of the country taken in possession by us, to her Majesty's use, and so to yours by her Majesty's grant, we thought good for the better assurance thereof to record some of the particular gentlemen and men of account, who then were present, as witnesses of the same; that thereby all occasion of cavil to the title of the country, in her Majesty's behalf may be prevented, which otherwise, such as like not the action may use and pretend. Their names are:

Master Philip	Captains
Master Arthur Barlow	
William Grenville	
John Wood	
James Bromwich	
Henry Green	
Benjamin Wood	
	Of the company
Simon Ferdinandez	
Nicholas Petman	
John Hewes	

We brought home also two of the savages being lusty men, whose names were Wanchese and Manteo.

8

SIR RICHARD GRENVILLE PLANTS THE FIRST VIRGINIA COLONY, 1585

The voyage made by Sir Richard Grenville, for Sir Walter Raleigh, to Virginia, in the year 1585.

The ninth day of April, in the year abovesaid, we departed from Plymouth, our fleet consisting of the number of seven sails. To wit, the *Tiger*, of the burden of seven score tons; a fly-boat called the *Roebuck* of the like burden; the *Lion* of a hundred tons or thereabouts; the *Elizabeth* of fifty tons, and the *Dorothy*, a small bark. To these were also adjoined for speedy services, two small pinnaces. The principal gentlemen of our company were these: Ralph Lane, Thomas Cavendish, John Arundell, Mr Raymond, Mr Stukeley, Mr Bromwich, Mr Vincent, Mr John Clarke, and divers others. Some were captains and others assistants for counsel and good directions in the voyage.

The fourteenth day of April we fell with Lancerota and Forteventura, isles of the Canaries. From thence we continued our course for Dominica, one of the Antilles of the West Indies, wherewith we fell the seventh day of May. The tenth day following we came to anchor at Cotesa, a little island situate near to the island of St John [San Juan], where we landed and refreshed ourselves all that day. The twelfth day of May we came to anchor in the bay of Mosquito, in the island of St John, within a falcon shot of the shore. Our general, Sir Richard Grenville, and the most part of our company landed, and began to fortify very near to the sea side. The river ran by one side of our fort, and the other two sides were environed with woods. The thirteenth day we began to build a new pinnace within the fort with the timber that we then felled in the country. Some part whereof we fetched three miles up in the land and brought it to our fort upon trucks, the Spaniard not daring to make or offer resistance. The sixteenth day there appeared unto us out of the woods eight horsemen of the Spaniards, about a quarter of a mile from our fort, staying about half an hour in viewing our forces. But as soon as they saw ten of our shot marching towards them, they presently retired into the woods.

The nineteenth day Master Cavendish, who had been separated from our fleet in a storm in the bay of Portugal, arrived at Cotesa within the sight of the *Tiger*. We thinking him afar off to have been either a Spaniard or French man of war, thought it good to weigh anchors, and to go room with him. This the *Tiger* did, and discerned him at last to be one of our consorts; for joy of whose coming our ships discharged their ordnance, and saluted him according to the manner of the seas.

The twenty-second day twenty other Spanish horsemen showed themselves to us upon the other side of the river. Seeing them, our general dispatched twenty footmen towards them and two horsemen of ours, mounted upon Spanish horses, which we before had taken in the time of our being on the island. They showed to our men a flag of truce and made signs to have a parley with us. Two of our men went half of the way upon the sands, and two of theirs came and met them. The two Spaniards offered very great salutations to our men, but began according to their Spanish proud humours, to expostulate with them about their arrival and fortifying in their country. They notwithstanding by our men's discreet answers were so cooled that, whereas they were told, that our principal intention was only to furnish ourselves with water and victuals and other necessaries, whereof we stood in need. We craved these might be yielded to us with fair and friendly means; otherwise our resolution was to practise force, and to relieve ourselves by the sword. The Spaniards in conclusion, seeing our men so resolute, yielded to our requests with large promises of all courtesy and great favour, and so our men and theirs departed.

The twenty-third day our pinnace was finished, and

launched. This done, our general with his captains and gentlemen marched up into the country about the space of four
miles. In a plain marsh they stayed expecting the coming of
the Spaniards, according to their promise, to furnish us with
victuals. They keeping their old custom for perjury and
breach of promise, came not. Whereupon our general fired
the woods thereabout, and so retired to our fort, which the
same day was fired also, and each man came aboard to be
ready to set sail the next morning.

The twenty-ninth day we set sail from St John's, being
many of us stung before upon shore with the mosquitoes.
The same night we took a Spanish frigate, which was forsaken
by the Spaniards upon the sight of us. The next day in the
morning very early we took another frigate with good and
rich freight and divers Spaniards of account in her. These
afterwards we ransomed for good round sums, and landed
them in St John's.

The twenty-sixth day our lieutenant master Ralph Lane
went in one of the frigates which we had taken, to Roxo bay
upon the southwest side of St John's, to fetch salt, being
thither conducted by a Spanish pilot. As soon as he arrived
there, he landed with his men to the number of twenty and
entrenched himself upon the sands immediately, compassing
one of their salt hills within the trench. Being seen of the
Spaniards, there came down towards him two or three troops
of horsemen and footmen, who gave him the looking and
gazing on, but durst not come near him to offer any resistance.
So master Lane in spite of their troops, carried their salt
aboard and laded his frigate and returned again to our fleet
the twenty-ninth day, which rode at St German's Bay. The
same day we all departed, and the next day arrived in the
island of Hispaniola. The first day of June we anchored at
Isabella, on the north side of Hispaniola. The third day of
June, the governor of Isabella and captain of the Port de Plata,
being certified by the reports of sundry Spaniards, who had
been well entertained aboard our ships by our general, that
in our fleet were many brave and gallant gentlemen who
greatly desired to see the governor, he thereupon sent gentle
commendations to our general, promising within few days
to come to him in person.

The fifth day the governor accompanied with a lusty friar and twenty other Spaniards, with their servants and negroes, came down to the seaside, where our ships rode at anchor. Our general manned immediately the most part of his boats with the chief men of our fleet, every man appointed and furnished in the best sort. At the landing of our general the Spanish Governor received him very courteously. The Spanish gentlemen saluted our English gentlemen, and their inferior sort did also salute our soldiers and seamen, liking our men, and likewise their qualities. At first they seemed to stand in fear of us and of so many of our boats, whereof they desired that all might not land their men. Yet in the end the courtesies that passed on both sides were so great that all fear and mistrust on the Spaniards' part was abandoned.

In the meantime while our English general and the Spanish governor discoursed betwixt them of divers matter, as of the state of the country, the multitude of the towns and people and the commodities of the island, our men provided two banqueting houses covered with green boughs; the one for the gentlemen, the other for the servants. A sumptuous banquet was brought in served by us all in plate, with the sound of trumpets and consort of music, wherewith the Spaniards were more than delighted.

The Spaniards, in recompense of our courtesy, caused a great herd of white bulls and oxen to be brought together from the mountains, and appointed for every gentleman and captain that would ride a horse ready saddled. They singled out three of the best of them to be hunted by horsemen after their manner, so that the pastime grew very pleasant for the space of three hours. All three of the beasts were killed, whereof one took the sea and there was slain with a musket. After this sport many rare presents and gifts were given and bestowed on both parts. The next day we played the merchants in bargaining with them by way of truck and exchange of divers of their commodities – horses, mares, kine, bulls, goats, swine, sheep, bull-hides, sugar, ginger, pearl, tobacco, and such like commodities of the island.

The seventh day we departed with great good will from the Spaniards from the island of Hispaniola. But the wiser sort do impute this great show of friendship and courtesy used towards us by the Spaniards rather to the force that we were of, and the vigilance and watchfulness that was amongst us, than to any hearty good will. For doubtless if they had been stronger than we, we might have looked for no better courtesy at their hands than Master John Hawkins received at St John de Ullua, or John Oxenham near the straits of Darien, and divers other of our countrymen in other places.

The eighth day we anchored at a small island to take seals, which in that place we understood to have been in great quantity. Here the general and certain others with him in the pinnace were in very great danger to have been all cast away; but by the help of God they escaped the hazard, and returned aboard the Admiral in safety.

The ninth day we arrived and landed in the isle of Caicos, in which island we searched for salt-ponds, upon the information of a Portuguese. He indeed abused our general and us, deserving a halter for his hire, if it had so pleased us. The twelfth we anchored at Guanima, and landed. The fifteenth and sixteenth we anchored and landed at Cyguateo. The twentieth we fell with the main of Florida. The twenty-third we were in great danger of wreck on a beach called the Cape of Fear. The twenty-fourth we came to anchor in a harbour, where we caught in one tide so much fish as would have yielded us twenty pounds in London. This was our first landing in Florida.

The twenty-sixth we came to anchor at Wococon. The twenty-ninth we weighed anchor to bring the *Tiger* into the harbour, where through the unskilfulness of the master whose name was Fernandez, the Admiral struck on ground, and sank. The third of July we sent word of our arriving at Wococon, to Wingina at Roanoke. The sixth Mr John Arundell was sent to the mainland, and Manteo with him. Captain Aubrey and captain Bonython the same day were sent to Croatoan, where they found two of our men left there with thirty others by captain Raymond, some twenty days before. The eighth captain Aubrey and captain Bonython returned, with two of our men found by them, to us at Wococon.

The eleventh day the general accompanied in his tilt boat with master John Arundell, master Stukeley, and divers other gentlemen, master Lane, master Cavendish, master Hariot, and twenty others in the new pinnace; captain Amadas, captain Clarke, with ten others in a shipboat; Francis Brooke and John White in another shipboat. They passed over the water from Wococon to the mainland victualled for eight days. In this voyage we first discovered the towns of Pomeiok, Aquascogoc and Secotan, and also the great lake called by the savages Paquipe, with divers other places, and so returned with that discovery to our fleet. The twelfth we came to the town of Pomeiok. The thirteenth we passed by water to Aquascogok. The fifteenth we came to Secotan, and were well entertained there by the savages. The sixteenth we returned thence, and one of our boats with the Admiral was sent to Aquascogok, to demand a silver cup which one of the savages had stolen from us. Not receiving it according to his promise, we burnt and spoiled their corn and town, all the people being fled.

The eighteenth we returned from the discovery of Secotan, and the same day came aboard our fleet riding at Wococon. The twenty-first our fleet anchoring at Wococon, we weighed anchor for Hatorask. The twenty-seventh our fleet anchored at Hatorask, and there we rested.

The twenty-ninth Irangino, brother to king Wingina, came aboard the Admiral, and Manteo with him. The second of August the Admiral was sent to Weapomeiok. The fifth Mr John Arundell was sent to England. The twenty-fifth our general weighed anchor, and set sail for England.

About the thirty-first he took a Spanish ship of 300 tons richly loaded, boarding her with a boat made with boards of chests, which fell asunder and sank at the ship's side, as soon as ever he and his men were out of it. The tenth of September, by foul weather the general, then shipped in the prize, lost sight of the *Tiger*. The sixth the *Tiger* fell with the Land's End, and the same day came to anchor at Falmouth. The eighteenth the general came with the prize to Plymouth, and was courteously received by divers of his worshipful friends.

The names of some gentlemen and others that remained one whole year in Virginia, under the government of master Ralph Lane.

Master Philip Amadas, Admiral of the country
Master Hariot
Master Acton
Master Edward Stafford
Thomas Luddington
Master Marvyn
Master Gardiner
Captain Vaughan
Master Kendall
Master Prideaux
Robert Holecroft
Rhys Courtney
Richard Gilbert
Steven Pomeroy
Master Hugh Rogers
Master Thomas Harvey
Master Snelling
Master Anthony Rouse
Master Allen
Master Michael Poleson

9

LANE'S REPORT OF VIRGINIA, 1585

*An extract of Master Ralph Lane's letter to Richard Hakluyt, Esquire,
and another gentleman of the middle Temple, from Virginia.*

Meanwhile you shall understand that since Sir Richard Grenville's departure from us, as also before, we have discovered
the mainland to be the goodliest soil under the cope of heaven.
So abounding with sweet trees that bring such sundry rich
and pleasant gums, grapes of such greatness, yet wild, as
France, Spain nor Italy have no greater; so many sorts of
apothecary drugs, such several kinds of flax, one kind like
silk, the same gathered of a grass as common there as grass
is here. Within these few days we have found here maize or
guinea wheat, whose ear yields corn for bread four hundred
upon one ear; the cane makes very good and perfect sugar;
also *Terra Samia*, otherwise pottery clay. Besides that, it is
the goodliest and most pleasing territory of the world; for
the continent is of an huge and unknown greatness, very well
peopled and towned, though savagely; and the climate so
wholesome that we had not one sick since we touched the
land here.

To conclude, if Virginia had but horses and oxen in some
reasonable proportion, I dare assure myself, being inhabited
with English, no realm in Christendom were comparable to
it. For this already we find, that what commodities soever
Spain, France, Italy, or the East parts do yield unto us, in
wines of all sorts, in oils, in flax, in resin, pitch, frankincense,
currants, sugars and such like, these parts do abound with the
growth of them all. But being savages that possess the land,
they know no use of the same. Sundry other rich commodities

that no parts of the world, be they West or East Indies, have
here we find great abundance of. The people naturally are
most courteous, and very desirous to have clothes, but especially of coarse cloth rather than silk; coarse canvas they
also like well of, but copper carries the price of all, so it be
made red. Thus, good Mr Hakluyt and Mr H., I have joined
you both in one letter of remembrance, as two that I love
dearly well, and, commending me most heartily to you both,
I commit you to the tuition of the Almighty. From the new
Fort in Virginia, this third of September, 1585.

Your most assured friend,
Ralph Lane

10

THE FIRST VIRGINIA COLONY, 1585–6

An account of the particularities of the employments of the Englishmen left in Virginia by Sir Richard Grenville under the charge of master Ralph Lane, general of the same, from the seventeenth of August 1585 until the eighteenth of June 1586 at which time they departed the country: sent and directed to Sir Walter Raleigh.

That I may proceed with order in this discourse, I think it requisite to divide it into two parts. The first shall declare the particularities of such parts of the country within the mainland, as our weak number and supply of things necessary did enable us to enter into the discovery of.

The second part shall set down the reasons generally moving us to resolve on our departure at the instant with the general, Sir Francis Drake, and our common request for passage with him; when the barks, pinnaces, and boats with the masters and mariners meant by him to be left in the country, for the supply of such as for a further time meant to have stayed there, were carried away with tempest and foul weather. In the beginning whereof shall be declared the conspiracy of Pemisapan, with the savages of the mainland to have cut us off, &c.

The first part declaring the particularities of the country of Virginia

First therefore touching the particularities of the country, you shall understand that our discovery of the same has been extended from the island of Roanoke (the same having been the place of our settlement or inhabitation), into the south, into the North, into the north-west, and into the west.

The uttermost place to the southward of any discovery was Secotan, being by estimation four score miles distant from Roanoke. The passage from thence was through a broad sound within the mainland, the same being full of flats and shoals. We had but one boat with four oars to pass through the same, which boat could not carry above fifteen men with their furniture, baggage, and victual for seven days at the most. As for our pinnace, besides that she drew too deep water for that shallow sound, she would not stir for an oar. For these and other reasons (winter also being at hand) we thought good wholly to leave the discovery of those parts until our stronger supply.

To the northward our furthest discovery was to the Chesapians, distant from Roanoke about a hundred and thirty miles. The passage to it was very shallow and most dangerous, by reason of the breadth of the Sound, and the little succour that upon any storm was there to be had. But the territory and soil of the Chesapians (being distant fifteen miles from the shore) was for pleasantness of seat, for temperature of climate, for fertility of soil, and for the commodity of the sea, besides multitude of bears (being an excellent good victual) with great woods of sassafras, and walnut trees, is not to be excelled by any other whatsoever. There by sundry kings, whom they call *weroances*, and countries of great fertility adjoining to the same, as the Mandoages, Tripanicks, and Opossians, which all came to visit the colony of the English, which I had for a time appointed to be resident there.

To the north-west the farthest place of our discovery was to Chawanook, distant from Roanoke about a hundred and thirty miles. Our passage thither lies through a broad sound, but all fresh water, and the channel of a great depth, navigable for good shipping, but out of the channel full of shoals. The towns about the water's side situated by the way are these following: Passaquenoke, the women's town, Chepanoc, Weapomeiok, Muscamunge, and Metackwem: all these being under the jurisdiction of the king of Weopomeiok, called Okisco. From Muscamunge we enter into the river and jurisdiction of Chawanook. There the river begins to straighten until it comes to Chawanook, and then grows to be as narrow as the Thames between Westminster and Lambeth. Between Muscamunge and Chawanook, upon the left hand as we pass thither, is a goodly high land. There is a town which we called the Blind Town, but the savages called it Ohanoke, and has a very goodly cornfield belonging unto it. It is subject to Chawanook.

Chawanook itself is the greatest province and seigniory lying upon that river; and the very town itself is able to put seven hundred fighting men into the field, besides the force of the province itself. The king of the said province is called Menatonon, a man impotent in his limbs, but otherwise for a savage, a very grave and wise man. He is of a very singular good discourse in matters concerning the state, not only of his own country and the disposition of his own men, but also of his neighbours round about him as well far as near, and of the commodities that each country yields. When I had him prisoner with me for two days that we were together, he gave me more understanding and light of the country than I had received by all the searches and savages that before I or any of my company had had conference with. It was in March last past 1586. Amongst other things he told me that going three days' journey in a canoe up his river of Chawanook, and then descending to the land, you are within four days' journey to pass over land northeast to a certain king's country. This province lies upon the sea; but his place of greatest strength is an island situate, as he described unto me, in a bay, the water round about the island very deep.

Out of this bay he signified unto me that this king had so great quantity of pearl, and does so ordinarily take the same, as that not only his own skins that he wears, and the better sort of his gentlemen and followers are full set with the said pearl, but also his beds and houses are garnished with them. He has such quantity of them that it is a wonder to see.

He showed me that the said king was with him at Chawanook two years before, and brought him certain pearl, but the same of the worst sort. Yet was he glad to buy them of him for copper at a dear rate, as he thought. He gave me a rope of the same pearl, but they were black, and naught, yet many of them were very great, and a few amongst a number very orient and round. All which I lost with other things of mine, coming aboard Sir Francis Drake's fleet. Yet he told me that the said king had great store of pearls that were white, great, and round. His black pearls his men did take out of shallow water, but the white pearls his men fished for in very deep water.

It seemed to me by his speech that the said king had traffic with white men that had clothes as we have, for these white pearls. That was the reason he would not part with other than with black pearls, to those of the same country.

The kind of Chawanook promised to give me guides to go overland into that king's country whensoever I would. But he advised me to take good store of men with me, and good store of victual, for he said that king would be loath to suffer any strangers to enter into his country, and especially to meddle with the fishing for any pearl there. He was able to make a great many of men into the field, who he said would fight very well.

Hereupon I resolved with myself that if your supply had come before the end of April, and that you had sent any store of boats or men, to have had them made in any reasonable time, with a sufficient number of men and victuals to have found us until the new corn were come in, I would have sent a small bark with two pinnaces about by sea to the northward to have found out the bay he spoke of, and to have sounded the bar if there were any. This should have ridden there in the said bay about that island, while I with all the small boats I could make and with two hundred men, would have gone up to the head of the river of Chawanook with the guides that Menatonon would have given me. These I would have been assured should have been of his best men (for I had his best beloved son prisoner with me), who also should have kept me company in an handlock with the rest, foot by foot, all the voyage overland.

My meaning was further at the head of the river in the place of my descent, where I would have left my boats, to have raised a sconce with a small trench and a palisade upon the top of it. In this and in the guard of my boats I would have left five-and-twenty or thirty men. With the rest would I have marched with as much victual as every man could have carried, with their furniture, mattocks, spades and axes, two

days' journey. In the end of my march upon some convenient
plot would I have raised another sconce according to the
former, where I would have left fifteen or twenty. And if it
would have fallen out conveniently, in the way I would have
raised my said sconce upon some cornfield, that my company
might have lived upon it.

And so I would have held this course of ensconcing every
two days' march, until I had arrived at the bay or port he
spoke of. Finding this to be worth the possession, I would
there have raised a main fort, both for the defence of the
harbour and our shipping also, and would have reduced our
whole habitation from Roanoke and from the harbour there
(which by proof is very naught) unto this other before mentioned. In the four days' march before specified could I at all
times return with my company back unto my boats riding
under my sconce, very near whereunto directly from the west
runs a most notable river, and in all those parts most famous,
called the river of Moratoc. This river opens into the broad
sound of Weapomeiok. The river of Chawanook and all the
other sounds and bays, salt and fresh, show no current in
the world in calm weather, but are moved altogether with
the wind. But this river of Moratoc has so violent a current
from the west and southwest that it made me almost of
opinion that with oars it would scarce be navigable. It passes
with many creeks and turnings, and for the space of thirty
miles rowing and more, it is as broad as the Thames betwixt
Greenwich and the Isle of Dogs, in some place more and in
some less. The current runs as strong, being entered so high
into the river, as at London Bridge upon ebb-tide.

Not only Menatonon but also the savages of Moratoc
themselves do report strange things of the head of that river,
and that from Moratoc itself, which is a principal town upon
that river, it is thirty days' – as some of them say and some
say forty days' – voyage to the head thereof. This head,
they say, springs out of a main rock in that abundance that
forthwith it makes a most violent stream. This huge rock
stands so near unto a sea that many times in storms (the wind
coming outwardly from the sea) the waves thereof are beaten
into the said fresh stream, so that the fresh water for a certain
space, grows salt and brackish. I took a resolution with

myself, having dismissed Menatonon upon a ransom agreed for, and sent his son into the pinnace to Roanoke, to enter presently so far into that river with two double wherries, and forty persons one or other, as I could have victual to carry us. Until we could meet with more either of the Moratoks, or of the Mangoaks, who are another kind of savages, dwelling more to the westward of the said river. But the hope of recovering more victual from the savages made me and my company as narrowly to escape starving in that discovery before our return, as ever men did that missed the same.

Pemisapan, who had changed his name of Wingina upon the death of his brother Granganimeo, had given both the Choanists, and Mangoaks word of my purpose touching them, I having been enforced to make him privy to the same, to be served by him of a guide to the Mangoaks. Yet he did never rest to solicit continually my going upon them, certifying me of a general assembly even at that time made by Menatonon at Chawanook of all his weroances and allies to the number of three thousand bows, preparing to come upon us at Roanoke. The Mangoaks also were joined in the same confederacy, who were able of themselves to bring as many more to the enterprise. And true it was that at that time the assembly was held at Chawanook about us, as I found at my coming thither; which unlooked for did so dismay them, as it made us have the better hand at them. But this confederacy against us of the Choanists and Mangoaks was altogether and wholly procured by Pemisapan himself, as Menatonon confessed unto me. He sent them continual word that our purpose was fully bent to destroy them; on the other side he told me that they had the like meaning towards us.

He in like sort sent word to the Mangoaks of my intention to pass up into their river, and to kill them (as he said). Both they and the Moratoks, with whom before we were entered into a league, and they had ever dealt kindly with us, abandoned their towns along the river, and retired themselves with their women and their corn within the mainland. In three days' voyage up the river we could not meet a man nor find a grain of corn in any of their towns. I considered with myself that we had but two days' victual left and that we were then a hundred and sixty miles from home, besides

casualty of contrary winds or storms, and suspected treason
of our own savages in the discovery of our voyage intended
– though we had no intention to be hurtful to any of them,
otherwise than for our copper to have had corn of them. I at
night upon the corps of guard, before the putting forth of
sentinels, advertised the whole company of the case we stood
in for victual, and of my opinion that we were betrayed by
our own savages, and of purpose drawn forth by them upon
vain hope to be in the end starved. Seeing all the country fled
before us, and therefore while we had those two days' victual
left, I thought it good for us to make our return homeward.
It was necessary for us to get the other side of the sound of
Weopomeiok in time, where we might be relieved upon the
weirs of Chipanum, and the women's town, although the
people were fled.

Thus much I signified unto them, as the safest way. Nevertheless I did refer it to the greatest number of voices, whether
we should adventure the spending of our whole victual in
some further view of that most goodly river in hope to meet
with some better hap, or otherwise to retire ourselves back
again. That they might be the better advised, I willed them
to deliberate all night upon the matter, and in the morning at
our going aboard to set our course according to the desires
of the greatest part. Their resolution fully and wholly was
(and not three found to be of the contrary opinion) that, while
there was left but one half pint of corn for a man, we should
not leave the search of that river. There were in the company
two mastiffs, upon the pottage of which with sassafras leaves
(if the worst fell out) the company would make shift to live
two days. This time would bring them down the current to
the mouth of the river and to the entry of the sound. In two
days more at the farthest they hoped to cross the sound and
to be relieved by the weirs, which two days they would fast
rather than be drawn back a foot till they had seen the
Mangoaks, either as friends or foes. This resolution of theirs
did not a little please me, since it came of themselves, although
for mistrust of that which afterwards did happen, I pretended
to have been rather of the contrary opinion.

That which made me most desirous to have some doings
with the Mangoaks either in friendship or otherwise to have

had one or two of them prisoners, was, for that it is a thing most notorious to all the country, that there is a province to which the Mangoaks have recourse and traffic up that river of Moratoc, which has a marvellous and most strange mineral. This mine is so notorious amongst them, as not only to the savages dwelling up the river, and also the savages of Chawanook, and all them to the westward, but also to all them of the mainland. The country's name is of fame, and is called Chaunis Temoatan.

The mineral they say is *wassador*, which is copper; but they call by the name of *wassador* every metal whatsoever. They say it is of the colour of our copper, but our copper is better than theirs; the reason is that it is redder and harder, whereas that of Chaunis Temoatan is very soft and pale. They say that they take the said metal out of a river that falls very swift from high rocks and hills, and they take it in shallow water. The manner is this. They take a great bowl, by their description as great as one of our shields, and wrap a skin over the hollow part thereof, leaving one part open to receive the mineral. That done, they watch the coming down of the current and the change of the colour of the water, then suddenly chop down the said bowl with the skin, and receive into the same as much ore as will come in. This is ever as much as their bowl will hold, which presently they cast into a fire. Forthwith it melts, and does yield in five parts, at the first melting, two parts of metal for three parts of ore.

Of this metal the Mangoaks have so great store, by report of all the savages adjoining, that they beautify their houses with great plates of the same. This to be true I received by report of all the country, and particularly by young Skiko, the king of Chawanook's son my prisoner, who also himself had been prisoner with the Mangoaks, and set down all the particularities to me before mentioned. But he had not been at Chaunis Temoatan himself; for, he said, it was twenty days' journey overland from the Mangoaks, to the said mineral country and that they passed through certain other territories between them and the Mangoaks, before they came to the said country.

I was very inquisitive in all places where I came to take very particular information, by all the savages that dwelt towards those parts, and especially of Menatonon himself, who in everything did very particularly inform me. He promised me guides of his own men, who should pass over with me, even to the said country of Chaunis Temoatan. Overland from Chawanook to the Mangoaks is but one day's journey from sun rising to sun setting; whereas by water it is seven days with the soonest. These things made me very desirous by all means possible to recover the Mangoaks, and to get some of their copper for an assay, and therefore I willingly yielded to their resolution.

But it fell very contrary to all expectation, and likelihood. After two days' travel and our whole victual spent, lying on shore all night, we could never see man – only fires we might perceive made along the shore where we were to pass, and up into the country – until the very last day. In the evening whereof, about three of the clock we heard certain savages call, as we thought, Manteo. He was also at that time with me in the boat, whereof we all being very glad, hoping of some friendly conference with them, and making him to answer them, they presently began a song, as we thought, in token of our welcome to them. But Manteo at once betook him to his piece, and told me that they meant to fight with us. This word was not so soon spoken by him, and the light wherry ready to put to shore, but there lighted a volley of their arrows among them in the boat, but did no hurt (God be thanked) to any man. Immediately, the other lying ready with their shot to scour the place for our hand weapons to land upon, which was presently done – although the land was very high and steep – the savages forthwith quitted the shore, and betook themselves to flight.

We landed, and fair and easily followed for a small time after them, who had wooded themselves we know not where. The sun drawing then towards the setting, and being assured that the next day if we would pursue them, though we might happen to meet with them, yet we should be assured to meet with none of their victual, which we then had good cause to think of. Therefore choosing for the company a convenient ground in safety to lodge in for the night, making a strong corps of guard, and putting out good sentinels, I determined the next morning before the rising of the sun to be going back again, if possibly we might recover the mouth of the river, into the broad Sound. At my first motion I found my whole company ready to assent; for they were now come to their dogs' porridge, that they had bespoken for themselves if that befell them which did, and I before mistrust we should hardly escape.

The end was we came the next day by night to the river's mouth within four or five miles of the same, having rowed in one day down the current, as much as in four days we had done against the same. We lodged upon an island, where we had nothing in the world to eat but pottage of sassafras leaves, the like whereof for a meat was never used before as I think. The broad sound we had to pass the next day all fresh and fasting. That day the wind blew so strongly, and the billow so great, that there was no possibility of passage without sinking of our boats. This was upon Easter eve, which was fasted very truly. Upon Easter day in the morning, the wind coming very calm, we entered the sound, and by four of the clock we were at Chipanum, whence all the savages that we had left there were fled. But their weirs did yield us some fish, as God was pleased not utterly to suffer us to be lost; for some of our company were far spent. The next morning we arrived at our home Roanoke.

I have set down this voyage somewhat particularly, to the end it may appear unto you (as true it is) that there wanted no great good will from the most to the least among us, to have performed this discovery of the mine. For the discovery of a good mine, by the goodness of God, or a passage to the South Sea, or some way to it, and nothing else can bring this country in request to be inhabited by our nation. With the discovery of either of the two above showed, it will be the most sweet and healthful climate, and the most fertile soil (being manured) in the world. Then will sassafras and many other roots and gums there found make good merchandise and lading for shipping; which otherwise of themselves will not be worth the fetching.

Provided also, that there be found out a better harbour than yet there is, which must be to the northward, if any there be. This was my intention to have spent this summer in the search of, and of the mine of Chaunis Temoatan. The one I would

have done, if the barks that I should have had of Sir Francis
Drake, by his honourable courtesy, had not been driven away
by storm. The other, if your supply of more men and some
other necessaries had come to use in any convenient sufficiency. For this river of Moratok promises great things, and
by the opinion of Mr Hariot the head of it by the description
of the country, either rises from the bay of Mexico, or else
from very near unto the same, that opens out into the South
Sea.

And touching the mineral, thus does Mr Joachim affirm,
that though it be but copper, seeing the savages are able to
melt it, it is one of the richest minerals in the world.

Wherefore a good harbour found to the northward, and
from thence four days overland to the river of Choanok,
sconces being raised; from whence again overland through
the province of Choanok one day's voyage to the first town
of the Mangoaks up the river of Moratok, you shall clear
yourself from all those dangers and broad shallow sounds
before mentioned; and gain within four days' travel into the
heart of the mainland two hundred miles at the least, with far
greater felicity than otherwise can be performed.

Thus, sir, I have though simply, yet truly set down unto
you, what my labour with the rest of the gentlemen and poor
men of our company (not without both pain and peril) could
yield unto you. This might have been performed in more
perfection, if only that which you have provided for us had
at the first been left with us. Or if it has not been for the
carrying away, by a most strange and unlooked for storm,
of all our provision, with barks, master, mariners, and sundry
also of my own company. All had been so courteously
supplied by the general Sir Francis Drake, the same having
been most sufficient to have performed the greatest part of
the premises, which must ever make me to think the hand of
God only (for some good purpose to myself yet unknown)
to have been in the matter.

*The second part touching the conspiracy of Pemisapan, the discovery of the
same, and at the last, of our request to depart with Sir Francis Drake for
England*

Ensenore a savage, father to Pemisapan, being the only friend to our nation that we had amongst them, and about the king, died the twentieth of April 1586. He alone had before opposed himself in their consultations against all matters proposed against us, which both the king and all the rest of them after Granganimeo's death, were very willing to have preferred. And he was not only during his life, a means to save us from hurt, as poisonings and such like, but also to do us very great good, and singularly in this.

The king was advised and of himself disposed, as a ready means to have assuredly brought us to ruin in the month of March 1586, himself with all his savages to have run away from us, and to have left his ground in the island unsowed. If he had done this, there had been no possibility in common reason (but by the immediate hand of God) that we could have been preserved from starving out of hand. For at that time we had no weirs for fish, neither had our men skill of the making of them, neither had we one grain of corn for seed to put into the ground.

In my absence on my voyage to the Choanists, and Mangoaks, they had raised a rumour among themselves, that I and my company were part slain, and part starved by the Choanists, and Mangoaks. One part of this tale was too true, that I and mine were like to be starved, but the other false. Nevertheless, until my return it took such effect in Pemisapan's breast, and in those against us, that they grew not only into contempt of us, but also (contrary to their former reverend opinion in show, of the Almighty God of heaven, and Jesus Christ whom we serve and worship, whom before they would acknowledge and confess the only God) now they began to blaspheme. They flatly said that our Lord God was not God, since he suffered us to sustain much hunger, and also to be killed by the Renapoaks, for so they call by that general name all the inhabitants of the whole mainland, of what province soever. Insomuch as neither old Ensenore, nor any of his fellows, could for his sake have any more credit for us; and it came so far that the king was resolved to have presently gone away as is aforesaid.

But even in the beginning of this rumour I returned. When he saw, contrary to his expectation, that not only myself and my company were all safe, but also by report of his own three savages who had been with me besides Manteo in that voyage; that the Choanists and Mangoaks (whose name and multitude besides their valour are terrible to all the rest of the provinces) durst not abide us, and that those that did abide us were killed; and that we had taken Menatonon prisoner and brought his son that he best loved to Roanoke with me, it did not a little assuage all devices against us. On the other side, it made Ensenore's opinions to be received again with greater respect. For he had often before told them, and then renewed his former speeches, both to the king and the rest, that we were the servants of God, and that we were not subject to be destroyed by them. But contrarywise, that they amongst them that sought our destruction, should find their own, and not be able to work ours; and that we being dead men were able to do them more hurt than now we could do being alive. An opinion very confidently at this day held by the wisest amongst them, and of their old men. As also, that they have been in the night a hundred miles from any of us, in the air shot at and struck by some men of ours, that by sickness had died among them. Many of them hold opinion that we be dead men returned into the world and that we do not remain dead but for a certain time, and that then we return again.

All these speeches then again grew in full credit with them, the king, and all, when he saw the small troop returned, and in that sort from those whose very names were terrible unto them. But that which made up the matter on our side was an accident, yea rather (as all the rest was) the good providence of the Almighty for the saving of us.

Within certain days after my return Menatonon sent a messenger to visit his son, and sent me certain pearls for a present, or rather, as Pemisapan told me, for the ransom of his son. Therefore I refused them. But the greatest cause of his sending was to signify unto me that he had commanded Okisko, king of Weopomiok, to yield himself servant and homager to the great *weroanza* of England, and after her to Sir Walter Raleigh. To perform which commandment Okisko sent four-and-twenty of his principal men to Roanoke to Pemisapan, to signify that they were ready to perform the same, and to let me know that from that time forward he and his successors were to acknowledge her Majesty their only sovereign, and next unto her as is aforesaid.

All which being done, and acknowledged by them all, in the presence of Pemisapan his father, and all his savages in counsel then with him, it did for the time thoroughly (as it seemed) change him in disposition toward us. Forthwith Ensenore won this resolution of him that he should cause his men to set up weirs for us. Both which he went in hand with and did so labour the expedition of it that in the end of April he had sowed a good quantity of ground. So much as had been sufficient to have fed our whole company for a whole year. Besides that he gave us a certain plot of ground for ourselves to sow.

All which put us in marvellous comfort, if we could pass from April until the beginning of July (which was to have been the beginning of their harvest). Then a new supply out of England or else our own store would well enough maintain us. All our fear was of the two months betwixt; in which mean space if the savages should not help us with *cassavi* bread, and that our weirs should fail us (as often they did), we might very well starve. Notwithstanding the growing corn, like the starving horse in the stable, with the growing grass, as the proverb is: which we very hardly had escaped but only by the hand of God, as it pleased him to try us.

For within few days after Ensenore our friend died. He was no sooner dead but certain of our great enemies about Pemisapan, as Osacan a *weroance*, Tanaquiny and Wanchese most principally, were in hand to put their old practices in use against us. These were readily embraced, and all their former devices against us renewed. But that of starving us by their forbearing to sow was broken by Ensenore in his life, by having made the king to sow the ground, not only in the island, but also at Dasamonquepeio in the mainland within two leagues over against us. Nevertheless there wanted no store of mischievous practices among them, and of all they resolved principally of this following.

First that Okisko, king of Weopomeiok, with the Mandoaks should be moved with great quantity of copper entertained to the number of seven or eight hundred bows, to enterprise the matter thus to be ordered. They of Weopo-meiok should be invited to a certain kind of month's mind, which they solemnise in their savage manner for any great personage dead, and should have been for Ensenore. At this instant also should the Mandoaks, who were a great people, with the Chesapians and their friends to the number of seven hundred, be armed at a day appointed at Dasamonquepeio. There lying close at the sign of fires, which should inter-changeably be made on both sides, when Pemisapan with his troop should have executed me and some of our *weroances* (as they called all our principal officers), the main forces of the rest should have come over into the island. There they meant to have dispatched the rest of the company, whom they did imagine to find both dismayed and dispersed abroad in the island, seeking of crabs and fish to live on.

Tanaquiny and Andacon two principal men about Pemisa-pan and very lusty fellows, with twenty more appointed to them, had the charge of my person to see an order taken, which they meant should in this sort have been executed. In the dead time of the night they would have beset my house, and put fire in the reeds that the same was covered with. Meaning (as it was likely) that myself would have come running out of a sudden amazed in my shirt without arms. Upon the instant whereof they would have knocked out my brains.

The same order was given to certain of his fellows for Mr Hariot. So for all the rest of our better sort; all our houses at one instant being set on fire and that as well for them of the fort as for us at the town. Now to the end that we might be the fewer in number together, and so be the more easily dealt with (for indeed ten of us with our arms prepared, were a terror to a hundred of the best sort of them), they agreed and did immediately put it in practice that they should not for any copper sell us any victuals whatsoever. In the night they should send to have our weirs robbed and cause them to be broken, and once being broken never to be repaired again by them. By this means the king stood assured that I must be enforced for lack of sustenance to disband my company into sundry places to live upon shell-fish. For so the savages themselves do, going to Hatorask, Croatoan, and other places, fishing and hunting, while their grounds to be in sowing, and their corn growing. This failed not his expectation.

The famine grew so extreme among us, our weirs failing us of fish, that I was enforced to send captain Stafford with twenty with him to Croatoan, my lord Admiral's island to serve two turns in one: to feed himself and his company, and also to keep watch if any shipping came upon the coast to warn us of the same. I sent Mr Prideaux with the pinnace to Hatorask, and ten with him, with the provost marshal to live there, and also to wait for shipping. Also I sent every week sixteen or twenty of the rest of the company to the mainland over against us, to live off roots and oysters.

In the meanwhile Pemisapan went of purpose to Dasamonquepeio for three causes. The one to see his grounds there broken up and sowed for a second crop; the other to withdraw himself from my daily sending to him for supply of victual for my company. For he was afraid to deny me anything, neither durst he in my presence but by colour and with excuses. This I was content to accept for the time, meaning in the end, as I had reason, to give him the jump once for all. But in the meanwhile, as I had ever done before, I and mine bore all wrongs, and accepted all excuses.

My purpose was to have relied myself with Menatonon, and the Choanists, who in truth as they are more valiant people and in greater number than the rest, so are they more faithful in their promises. Since my late being there they had given many tokens of earnest desire they had to join in perfect league with us, and therefore were greatly offended with Pemisapan (and Weopomeiok) for making him believe such tales of us. The third cause of this going to Dasamonquepeio was to dispatch his messengers to Weopomeiok, and to the Mandoaks: all which he did with great imprest of copper in hand, making large promises to them of greater spoil.

The answer within few days after came from Weopomeiok, which was divided into two parts. First for the king Okisko, who denied to be of the party for himself or any of his especial followers, and therefore did immediately retire himself with his force into the mainland. The other was concerning the rest of the said province who accepted of it; and in like sort the Mandoaks received the imprest. The day of their assembly at Roanoke was appointed the tenth of June. All the premises were discovered by Skiko, the king Menatonon's son, my prisoner. Having once attempted to run away, I laid him in the bilboes, threatening to cut off his head, whom I remitted at Pemisapan's request. Whereupon he being persuaded that he was our enemy to the death, he did not only feed him with himself but also make him acquainted with all his practices. On the other side, the young man finding himself as well used at my hand as I had means to show, and that all my company made much of him, he flatly discovered all unto me. It also afterwards was revealed unto me by one of Pemisapan's own men, that night before he was slain.

These mischiefs being all instantly upon me and my company to be put in execution, it stood me in hand to study how to prevent them, and also to save all others, who were at that time so far from me. Whereupon I sent to Pemisapan to put suspicion out of his head, that I meant presently to go to Croatoan, for that I had heard of the arrival of our fleet (though I in truth had neither heard nor hoped for so good adventure). And that I meant to come by him to borrow of his men to fish for my company and to hunt for me at Croatoan; as also to buy some four days' provision to serve for my voyage.

He sent me word that he would himself come over to Roanoke, but from day to day he deferred, only to bring the Weopomeioks with him and the Mandoaks, whose time appointed was within eight days after. It was the last of May 1586 when all his own savages began to make their assembly at Roanoke, at his commandment sent abroad unto them. I resolved not to stay longer upon his coming over, since he meant to come with so good company, but thought good to go and visit him with such as I had, which I resolved to do the next day. But that night I meant by the way to give them in the island a surprise, and at the instant to seize upon all the canoes about the island, to keep him from advertisements.

But the town took the alarm before I meant it to them. The occasion was this. I had sent the master of the wherry, with a few with him, to gather up all the canoes in the setting of the sun and to take as many as were going from us to

Dasamonquepeio, but to suffer any that came from thence to land. He met with a canoe going from the shore, and over-threw the canoe, and cut off two savages' heads. This was not done so secretly but he was discovered from the shore. Whereupon the cry arose; for in truth they, privy to their own villainous purposes against us, held as good espial upon us, both day and night, as we did upon them.

The alarm given, they took themselves to their bows and we to our arms; some three or four of them at the first were slain with our shot, the rest fled into the woods. The next morning with the wherry and one canoe taking twenty-five with the colonel of the Chesapians and the sergeant-major, I went to Dasamonquepeio. Being landed, I sent Pemisapan word that I was going to Croatoan, and meant to take him in the way to complain unto him of Osocon, who the night past was conveying away my prisoner, whom I had there present tied in an handlock. Hereupon the king did abide my coming to him, and finding myself amidst seven or eight of his principal *weroances* and followers (not regarding any of the common sort), I gave the watchword agreed upon (which was, Christ our victory). Immediately those his chief men and himself had, by the mercy of God for our deliverance, that which they had purposed for us.

The king himself being shot through by the colonel with a pistol, lying on the ground for dead, and I looking as watchfully for the saving of Manteo's friends, as others were busy that none of the rest should escape – suddenly he started up and ran away as though he had not been touched. Insomuch as he overran all the company, being by the way shot thwart the buttocks by my Irish boy with my petronel. In the end an Irishman serving me, one Nugent, and the deputy provost, undertook him; and following him in the woods overtook him. I in some doubt lest we had lost both the king and my man by our own negligence to have been intercepted by the savages, we met him returning out of the woods with Pemisapan's head in his hand.

This fell out the first of June 1586, and the eighth of the same came advertisement to me from captain Stafford, lying at my lord admiral's island, that he had discovered a great fleet of three-and-twenty sails. But whether they were friends or foes he could not yet discern. He advised me to stand upon as good guard as I could. The ninth of the said month he himself came unto me, having that night before and that same day travelled by land twenty miles. I must truly report of him, he was the gentleman that never spared labour or peril either by land or water, fair weather or foul, to perform any service committed unto him. He brought me a letter from the general, Sir Francis Drake, with a most bountiful offer for the supply of our necessities to the performance of the action we were entered into – not only of victuals, munition and clothing, but also of barks, pinnaces, and boats; they also by him to be victualled, manned, and furnished to my contentation.

The tenth day he arrived in the road of our bad harbour. Coming there to an anchor, the eleventh day I came to him, whom I found in deeds most honourably to perform that which in writing he had most courteously offered. He had aforehand propounded the matter to all the captains of his fleet, and got their consent thereto. With such thanks unto him and his captains for his care both of us and of our action, I craved at his hands that it would please him to take with him into England a number of weak and unfit men for my good action; and in place of them to supply me of his company with oar-men, artificers, and others. That he would leave us so much shipping and victual as about August following would carry me and all my company into England – when we had discovered somewhat, that for lack of needful provision in time left with us as yet remained undone. That it would please him to leave some sufficient masters not only to carry us into England, when time should be, but also to search the coast for some better harbour, if there were any; and especially to help us to some small boats and oar-men. Also for a supply of calivers, hand weapon, match and lead, tools, apparel, and such like.

He received these my requests according to his usual commendable manner of government (as it was told me), calling his captains to counsel. The resolution was that I should send such of my officers of my company as I used in such matters, with their notes, to go aboard with him. These were the master of the victuals, the keeper of the store, and the vice-treasurer. He appointed forthwith for me *The Francis*, being a very proper bark of 70 tons, and took present order for bringing of victual aboard her for a hundred men for four months, with all my other demands whatsoever, to the uttermost.

Further, he appointed for me two pinnaces and four small boats: and he had gotten the full assents of two of as sufficient experienced masters as were any in his fleet, by judgement of them that knew them, with sufficient company to tarry with me – to employ themselves most earnestly in the action as I should appoint them, until the term which I promised of our return to England again. The names of one of those masters was Abraham Kendall, the other Griffith Herne.

While these things were in hand, the provision being brought and my masters being also gone aboard, and my own officers with others of my company with them (all which was dispatched by the general the twelfth of the month), the thirteenth of the same there arose such an unwonted storm and continued four days, that had like to have driven all on shore, if the Lord had not held his holy hand over them. The general had providently foreseen the worst himself, then about my dispatch putting himself aboard. But in the end, having driven sundry of the fleet to put to sea, *The Francis* also with all my provisions, my two masters, and my company aboard, she was seen to be free from the same and to put clear to sea.

This storm having continued from the thirteenth to the sixteenth of the month, and thus my bark put away, the general coming ashore made a new proffer unto me: a ship of 170 tons, called *The Bark Bonner*, with a sufficient master to tarry with me the time appointed, and victualled sufficiently to carry me and my company into England. But he would not for anything undertake to have her brought into our harbour; he was to leave her in the road, and to leave the care of the rest unto myself. He advised me to consider with my company of our case, and to deliver presently unto him in writing what I would require him to do for us.

Hereupon calling such captains and gentlemen of my company as then were at hand, their whole request was to me that, considering the case that we stood in, the weakness of our company, the small number of it, the carrying away of our first appointed bark with those two especial masters and our principal provisions, by the very hand of God as it seemed, stretched out to take us from thence. Considering also that his second offer, though most honourable of his part yet of ours not to be taken, insomuch as there was no possibility for her with any safety to be brought into the harbour; seeing furthermore, our hope for supply with Sir Richard Grenville, so undoubtedly promised us before Easter not yet come – neither then likely to come this year, considering the doings in England for Flanders, and also for America – that therefore I would resolve myself with my company to go into England in that fleet. Accordingly to make request to the general in all our names that he would be pleased to give us present passage with him. Which request of ours by myself delivered unto him he most readily assented unto. He sending immediately his pinnaces unto our island for the fetching away of a few that there were left with our baggage, the weather was so boisterous that the most of all we had, with all our cards, books and writings were by the sailors cast overboard, the greater number of the fleet being much aggrieved with their long and dangerous abode in that miserable road.

From whence the general in the name of the Almighty, weighing his anchors (having bestowed us among his fleet), for the relief of whom he had in that storm sustained more peril of wreck than in all his former most honourable actions against the Spaniards, with praises unto God for all, set sail the nineteenth of June 1586, and arrived in Portsmouth the seven-and-twentieth of July the same year.

11

HARIOT'S BRIEF AND TRUE REPORT OF THE NEW FOUND LAND OF VIRGINIA

A Brief and True Report of the new found land of Virginia; of the commodities there found and to be raised, as well merchantable as others. Written by Thomas Hariot, ★ *servant to Sir Walter Raleigh, a member of the Colony, and there employed in discovering a full twelvemonth.*

Ralph Lane, one of her Majesty's Esquires, and Governor of the Colony of Virginia, for the time there resident, to the gentle reader wishes all happiness in the Lord.

Albeit (gentle reader) the credit of the reports in this Treatise contained can little be furthered by the testimony of one as myself, through affection judged partial, though without desert – nevertheless, I have been requested by some particular friends to deliver freely my knowledge of the same. Thus much upon my credit I am to affirm, that things universally are so truly set down in this Treatise by the author thereof, an actor in the Colony, and a man no less for his honesty than learning commendable, as that I dare boldly avouch, it may very well pass with the credit of truth even among the most true relations of this age. Which I am ready any way with my word to acknowledge, so also (of the certainty thereof assured by my own experience) with this my public assertion I do affirm the same. Farewell in the Lord.

★ Thomas Hariot, 1506–1621, foremost mathematician and astronomer in Elizabethan England, for many years Raleigh's scientific adviser.

To the Adventurers, Favourers, and Well-willers of the enterprise for the inhabiting and planting in Virginia.

Since the first undertaking by Sir Walter Raleigh to deal in the action of discovering that country which is now called and known by the name of Virginia, many voyages having been thither made at sundry times to his great charge. First in the year 1584, and afterwards in the years 1585, 1586, and now of late this last year 1587. There have been divers and variable reports, with some slanderous speeches put abroad by many that returned from thence. Especially of that discovery which was made by the Colony transported by Sir Richard Grenville in the year 1585, being of all others the principal and as yet of most effect. The time of their abode in the country was a whole year, when in the other voyage before they stayed but six weeks; and the others after were only for supply and transportation, nothing more being discovered than had been before.

These reports have done not a little wrong to many that otherwise would have also favoured and adventured in the action, to the honour and benefit of our nation, besides the particular profit and credit which would redound to themselves. I hope by the sequel of events, to the shame of those that have avouched the contrary, it shall be manifest, if you the adventurers, favourers and well-willers do increase in number, or renew your good liking and furtherance to deal therein, according to the worthiness thereof already found, and as you shall understand hereafter to be requisite. Through cause of the diversity of realtions and reports many of your opinions could not be firm, nor the minds of some that are well disposed be settled in any certainty.

I have therefore thought it good, being one that have been in the discovery, and in dealing with the natural inhabitants specially employed; having therefore seen and known more than the ordinary, to impart so much unto you of the fruits of our labours as you may know how injuriously the enterprise is slandered, chiefly for two respects.

First, that some of you who are yet ignorant or doubtful may see that there is sufficient cause why the chief enterpriser,

with the favour of her Majesty, has not only continued
the action by sending into the country again and replanting
this last year a new Colony, but is also ready, according as
times and means will afford, to follow and prosecute the
same.

Secondly, that you knowing the continuance of the action,
by the view hereof you may learn what the country is, and
thereupon consider how your dealing therein may return you
profit and gain, be it either by inhabiting and planting, or
otherwise in furthering thereof.

Of our company that returned, some for their misdemean-
our and ill dealing in the country have been there worthily
punished. These by reason of their bad natures have ma-
liciously not only spoken ill of their governors, but for their
sakes slandered the country itself.

The cause of their ignorance was that they were of many
that were never out of the island* where we were seated, or
not far; or at least in few places else. Or of that many that,
after gold and silver were not so soon found as it was by them
looked for, had little or no care of any other thing but
to pamper their bellies. Or of that many who had little
understanding, less discretion, and more tongue than was
requisite. Some also were of a nice bringing up only in cities
or towns, or such as never had seen the world before. Because
there were not to be found any English cities nor such fair
houses, nor any of their old accustomed dainty food, nor any
soft beds of down or feathers, the country was to them
miserable and their reports according . . .

The Treatise whereof I will divide into three special parts.
In the first I will make declaration of such commodities there
already found or to be raised, which will not only serve the
ordinary turns of you who are and shall be the planters and
inhabitants, but such an overplus as by way of traffic and
exchange with England will enrich yourselves the providers.
Those that shall deal with you, the enterprisers to supply
them with most things which heretofore they have been
provided either by strangers or our enemies. These commodities, for distinction sake, I call Merchantable.

* Roanoke.

In the second I will set down all the commodites which we know the country by our experience yields of itself for victual and sustenance of man's life; such as are usually fed upon by the inhabitants of the country, as also by us during the time we were there.

In the last part I will mention such other commodities as I think behoveful for those that shall inhabit and plant there to know of; which specially concern building, as also some other necessary uses. With a brief description of the nature and manners of the people of the country.

The First Part of Merchantable Commodities

Silk of grass, or grass silk. There is a kind of grass in the country upon the blades whereof there grows very good silk in form of a thin glittering skin to be stripped off. It grows two foot and a half high or better; the blades are about two foot in length, and half an inch broad. The like grows in Persia, which is in the same climate as Virginia, of which many of the silk works that come from thence into Europe are made. If it be planted as in Persia, it cannot in reason be otherwise but that there will rise in short time great profit to the dealers therein seeing there is so great use and vent thereof as well in our country as elsewhere. By planting it in good ground, it will be far greater, better, and more plentiful; although there is great store thereof in many places of the country growing wild. This also by proof here in England, in making a piece of silk grogram, we found to be excellent good.

Worm silk. In many of our journeys we found silk-worms fair and great, as big as our ordinary walnuts. Although it has not been our hap to have found such plenty as elsewhere we heard of, yet seeing that the country naturally breeds them, there is no doubt but if art be added in planting mulberry trees, fit for their feeding and nourishing, there will rise as great profit in time to the Virginians as thereof does now to the Persians, Turks, Italians and Spaniards.

Flax and Hemp. The truth is that there is no great store in any one place together, by reason it is not planted but as soil yields of itself. There cannot be shown any reason but that it will grow there excellent well, and by planting will be yielded plentifully, seeing there is so much ground whereof some may well be applied to such purposes. What benefit hereof may grow in cordage and linens who cannot easily understand?

Alum. There is a vein of earth along the sea coast for the space of forty or fifty miles, whereof by the judgement of some that have made trial here in England, is made good alum, of that kind which is called Rock Alum. The same earth also yields white coppers, nitre, and alum; plume, but nothing so plentifully as common alum, which is also of price, and profitable.

Wapeih. A kind of earth so called by the natural inhabitants, very like to *Terra sigillata*. Having been refined, it has been found by some of our physicians and surgeons to be of the same kind of virtue, and more effectual. The inhabitants use it very much for the cure of sores and wounds. There is in divers places great plenty, and in some places of a blue sort.

Pitch, Tar, Resin and Turpentine. There are those kinds of trees which yield them abundantly and great store. In the very same island where we were seated, being fifteen miles in length and five or six miles in breadth, there are few trees else but of the same kind, the whole island being full.

Sassafras, called by the inhabitants Winauk, a kind of wood of pleasant and sweet smell, and of most rare virtues in physic for the cure of many diseases. It is found by experience to be far better and of more uses than the wood which is called *Guaiacum*, or *Lignum vitae*. For the description, the manner of using, and the manifold virtues thereof, I refer you to the book on Monardes, translated and entitled in English, *The Joyful News from the West Indies*.

Cedar. A very sweet wood and fine timber. If nests of chests be there made or timber thereof fitted for sweet and fine bedsteads, tables, desks, lutes, virginals, and many things else to make up freight with other principal commodities, will yield profit.

Wine. There are two kinds of grapes that the soil yields naturally; the one is small and sour, of the ordinary bigness as ours in England, the other far greater and luscious sweet.

When they are planted and husbanded as they ought, a principal commodity of wines by them may be raised.

Oil. There are two sorts of walnuts, both holding oil, the one far more plentiful than the other. When there are mills and other devices for the purpose, a commodity of them may be raised, because there is infinite store. There are also three several kinds of berries in the form of oak-acorns, which also by the experience of the inhabitants we find to yield very good sweet oil. Furthermore, the bears of the country are commonly very fat, and in some places there are many. Their fatness, because it is so liquid, may well be termed oil, and has many special uses.

Furs. All along the sea coast there is great store of otters, which being taken by weirs and other engines for the purpose, will yield good profit. We hope also of marten furs; by the relation of the people although there were but two skins that came to our hands. Wild cats also we have understanding of, although for the time we saw none.

Deer skins dressed after the manner of chamois, or undressed, are to be had of the natural inhabitants thousands yearly by way of traffic for trifles, and no more waste or spoil of deer than has been ordinarily in time before.

Civet-cats.* In our travels there was found one to have been killed by a savage or inhabitant, and in another place the smell where one or more had lately been before. Whereby we gather that there are some in the country: good profit will rise by them.

Iron. In two places of the country specially, one about 80 and the other 120 miles from the fort where we dwelt, we found near the water side the ground to be rocky, which by the trial of a mineral man was found to hold iron richly. It is found in many places of the country. It may be allowed for a good merchantable commodity, considering there the small charge for the labour and feeding of men, the infinite store of wood, the want of wood and dearness thereof in England, and the necessity of ballasting ships.

Copper. A hundred and fifty miles into the mainland in

---

* From which a perfume was extracted, much prized by Elizabethans: cf. Shakespeare, 'an ounce of civet'.

two towns we found with the inhabitants divers small plates of copper, that had been made by the inhabitants that dwell further into the country. There, they say, are mountains and rivers that yield also white grains of metal, which is to be deemed silver. For confirmation whereof I saw, with some others with me, two small pieces of silver grossly beaten about the weight of a sixpence, hanging in the ears of a *weroance* or chief lord that dwelt about eighty miles from us. I learned that it had come to his hands from the same place or near, where I after understood the copper was made, and the white grains of metal found. The aforesaid copper we also found by trial to hold silver.

Pearl. Sometimes in feeding on mussels we found some pearl; but it was our hap to meet with rags, or of a pied colour, not having yet discovered those places where we heard of better and more plenty. One of our company, a man of skill in such matters, had gathered together from among the savage people about five thousand. Of which number he chose so many as made a fair chain, which for their likeness and uniformity in roundness, orientness, and piedness of many excellent colours, with equality in greatness, were very fair and rare. These had therefore been presented to her Majesty, had we not through extremity of a storm lost them, with many things else in coming away from the country.

Sweet gums of divers kinds, and many other apothecary drugs. We will make special mention when we shall receive it from such men of skill in that kind that shall discover them more particularly than now I can make relation of, for want of the examples I had gathered and are now lost, with other things by casualty before mentioned.

Dyes of divers kinds. There is *shumach* well known, and used in England for black; the seed of an herb called *wasebur*, little small roots called *chappacor*, and the bark of the tree called by the inhabitants *tangomockonominge*: which dyes are for divers sorts of red. Their goodness for our English clothes remains yet to be proved. The inhabitants use them only for the dyeing of hair and colouring of their faces, and mantles made of deer skins. Also for the dyeing of rushes to make artistic works with in their mats and baskets. If they will not prove merchantable, the planters there shall find apt uses for them, as also for other colours which we know to be there.

Woad. A thing of so great vent and uses among English dyers, which can not be yielded sufficiently in our own country for spare of ground, maybe planted in Virginia, there being ground enough. The growth thereof need not to be doubted, when in the islands of the Azores it grows plentifully, which are in the same climate. So likewise of madder.

We carried thither sugar-canes to plant, which being not so well preserved as was requisite and the time of the year being past for their setting when we arrived, we could not make that proof of them we desired. Notwithstanding, seeing that they grow in the same climate in the south part of Spain and in Barbary, our hope in reason may yet continue. So likewise for oranges and lemons. There may be planted also quinces. Whereby may grow in reasonable time, if the action be diligently prosecuted, no small commodities in sugars, suckets, and marmalades.

Many other commodities by planting may there also be raised, which I leave to your discreet and gentle considerations: and many also may be there which yet we have not discovered.

The Second Part of such commodities as Virginia is known to yield for victual and sustenance of man's life, usually fed upon by the natural inhabitants; as also by us, during the time of our abode. And first of such as are sowed and husbanded

Pagatowr, a kind of grain so called by the inhabitants; the same in the West Indies is called maize: English men call it guinea-wheat, or turkey-wheat, according to the names of the countries from whence the like has been brought. The grain is about the bigness of our ordinary English peas, and not much different in form and shape, but of divers colours: some white, some red, some yellow, and some blue. All of them yield a very white and sweet flour; being used according to its kind, it makes very good bread. We made of the same in the country some malt, whereof was brewed as good ale as was to be desired. So likewise, by the help of hops, thereof may be made as good beer.

It is a grain of marvellous great increase: of a thousand, fifteen hundred, and some two thousand fold. There are three sorts, of which two are ripe in eleven and twelve weeks at the most; sometimes in ten, after the time they are set, and are then of height in stalk about six or seven foot. The other sort is ripe in fourteen, and is about ten foot high; of the stalks some bear four heads, some three, some one, and some two; every head containing five, six, or seven hundred grains, more or less. Of these grains, besides bread, the inhabitants make victual, either by parching them, or seething them whole until they are broken; or boiling the flour with water into a pap.

Okingier, called by us beans, because in greatness and partly in shape they are like to the beans in England, saving that they are flatter, of more diverse colours, and some pied. The leaf also of the stem is much different. In taste they are altogether as good as our English peas.

Wickonzowr, called by us peas, in respect of the beans for distinction sake, because they are much less, although in form they little differ; but in goodness of taste much like, and are far better than our English peas. Both the beans and peas are ripe in ten weeks after they are set. They make them victual either by boiling them all to pieces into a broth, or boiling them whole until they be soft and begin to break, as is used in England, either by themselves, or mixed together. Sometimes they mingle of wheat with them; sometimes also, being whole sodden, they bruise them in a mortar, and thereof make loaves of doughish bread, which they use to eat for variety.

Macocquer, according to their several forms, called by us pumpkins, melons, and gourds, because they are of the like forms as those kinds in England. In Virginia such of several forms are of one taste, and very good, and do also spring from one seed. There are of two sorts: one is ripe in the space of a month, and the other in two months.

There is an herb which in German is called *melden*. Some of those that I describe it unto take it to be a kind of spinach: it grows about four or five foot high. Of the seed thereof they make a thick broth, and pottage of a very good taste; of the stalk by burning into ashes they make a kind of salt earth, wherewith many use sometimes to season their broths. Other salt they know not. We ourselves used the leaves also for pot-herbs.

There is also another great herb in form of a marigold, about six foot in height, the head with the flour is a span in breadth. Some take it to be sunflower; of the seeds hereof they make both a kind of bread and broth.

All the aforesaid commodities for victual are set or sown, sometimes in grounds apart and severally by themselves; but for the most part together in one ground. The manner thereof, with the dressing and preparing of the ground, because I will note unto you the fertility of the soil, I think good briefly to describe.

The ground they never fatten with muck, dung, or any other thing, neither plough nor dig it as we in England, but only prepare it as follows. A few days before they sow or set, the men with wooden instruments made almost in form of mattocks or hoes with long handles; the women with short peckers or parers, because they use them sitting, of a foot long and about five inches in breadth, do only break the upper part of the ground to raise up the weeds, grass, and old stubs of corn stalks with their roots. This, after a day or two days' drying in the sun, being scraped up into many heaps, to save them labour for carrying them away, they burn into ashes. Whereas some may think that they use the ashes to better the ground, I say that then they would either disperse the ashes abroad, which we observed they do not except the heaps be too great, or else would take special care to set their corn where the ashes lie – which also we find they are careless of. And this is all the husbanding of their ground that they use.

Then their setting or sowing is after this manner. First for their corn, beginning in one corner of the plot, with a pecker they make a hole, wherein they put four grains, with care that they touch not one another (about an inch asunder) and cover them with the mould again. And so throughout the whole plot making such holes, and using them after such manner. But they be made in ranks, every rank differing from another half a fathom or a yard, and the holes also in every rank as much. There is a yard spare ground between every hole; where according to discretion here and there, they set as many beans and peas; in divers places also among the seeds of *macocquer, melden,* and sunflower.

The ground being thus set according to the rate by us experimented, and English acre containing forty perches in length and four in breadth, there yields in crops of corn, beans and peas, at the least two hundred London bushels, besides the *macocquer, melden,* and sunflower. Whenas in England forty bushels of our wheat yielded out of such an acre is thought to be much.

You who shall inhabit and plant there may know how specially that country corn is there to be preferred before ours. Besides, the manifold ways in applying it to victual, the increase is so much that small labour is needful in respect of that which must be used for ours. One man may prepare and husband so much ground (having once borne corn before) with less than twenty-four hours' labour, as shall yield him victual in a large proportion for a twelvemonth; the said ground being also but of twenty-five yards square. If need require, there might be raised out of one and the selfsame ground two harvests. For they sow or set, at any time when they think good, from the midst of March until the end of June; so that they also set when they have eaten of their first crop. In some places of the country they have two harvests, as we have heard, out of one and the same ground.

For English corn, whether to use or not to use it, you that inhabit may do as you shall have further cause to think best. Of the growth you need not doubt; for barley, oats, and peas, we have seen proof of, not being purposely sown but fallen casually in the worst sort of ground, and yet to be as fair as any we have ever seen here in England. But of wheat, because it was musty and had taken salt water, we could make no trial; and of rye we had none.

There is an herb which is sowed apart by itself, and is called by the inhabitants *Uppowoc.* In the West Indies it has divers names, according to the places and countries where it grows and is used. The Spaniards generally call it tobacco. The leaves thereof being dried and brought into powder, they take the fume or smoke thereof, by sucking it through pipes made of clay, into their stomach and head. Whence it purges superfluous phlegm and other gross humours, and opens all the pores and passages of the body. The use thereof not only preserves the body from obstructions, but also (if they have not been of too long continuance) in short time breaks them. Whereby their bodies are notably preserved in health, and know not many grievous diseases, wherewith we in England are often times afflicted.

This *uppowoc* is of so precious estimation among them that they think their gods are marvellously delighted therewith. Whereupon sometimes they make hallowed fires and cast some of the powder therein for a sacrifice. Being in a storm upon the waters, to pacify their gods they cast some up into the air and into the water. So a weir for fish being newly set up, they cast some therein and into the air; after an escape of danger, they cast some into the air likewise. But all done with strange gestures, stamping, sometimes dancing, clapping of hands, holding up of hands, and staring up into the heavens, uttering therewith, and chattering strange words and noises.

We ourselves, during the time we were there, used to suck it after their manner, as also since our return, and have found many rare and wonderful experiments of the virtues thereof. The use of it by so many of late, men and women of great calling, as else some learned physicians also, is sufficient witness.

These are all the commodities for sustenance of life that I can remember they use to husband; all else that follow are found growing naturally or wild.

Of Roots

Openauk are a kind of roots of round form, some of the bigness of walnuts, some far greater, which are found in moist and marsh grounds growing many together one by another in ropes, as though they were fastened with a string. Being boiled or sodden, they are very good meat. Monardes calls these roots, beads or *Pater nostri* of Santa Helena.

Okeepenauk are also of round shape, found in dry grounds: some are of the bigness of a man's head. They are to be eaten as they are taken out of the ground: for by reason of their dryness they will neither roast nor seethe. Their taste is not so good as of the former roots; notwithstanding for want of bread and sometimes for variety, the inhabitants eat them with fish or flesh, and in my judgement they do as well as the household bread made of rye here in England.

Kaishucpenauk, a white kind of roots about the bigness of hen's eggs, and near of that form; their taste was not so good to our seeming as of the other. The inhabitants notwithstanding used to boil and eat many.

Tsinaw, a kind of root much like unto that which in England is called the China root brought from the East Indies. And we know not but that it may be of the same kind. These roots grow many together in great clusters, and do bring forth a brier stalk, but the leaf in shape far unlike: being supported by the trees it grows nearest unto, it it will reach or climb to the top of the highest. From these roots while they be new or fresh, being chopped into small pieces and stamped, is strained with water a juice that makes bread; also, being boiled, a very good spoonmeat in manner of a jelly, and is much better in taste if it be tempered with oil. This *tsinaw* is not of that sort which by some was caused to be brought into England for the China root; for it was discovered since, and is in use. But that which was brought hither is not yet known, neither by us nor by the inhabitants, to serve for any use or purpose, although the roots in shape are very like.

Coscushaw some of our company took to be that kind of root which the Spaniards in the West Indies call cassava. It grows in very muddy pools and moist grounds. Being dressed according to the country manner, it makes a good bread and also a good spoonmeat, and is used very much by the inhabitants. The juice of this root is poison, and therefore heed must be taken before anything be made therewith. Either the roots must be first sliced and dried in the sun, or by the fire and then, being crushed into flour, will make good bread; or else while they are green they are to be pared, cut in pieces, and stamped. Loaves of the same to be laid near or over the fire until it be sour. Being well beaten again, bread or spoonmeat very good in taste and wholesome may be made thereof.

Habascon is a root of hot taste, almost of the form and bigness of a parsnip; of itself it is no victual, but only a help, being boiled together with other meats.

There are also leeks, differing little from ours in England, that grow in many places of the country; of which, when we came in places where they were, we gathered and ate many, but the natural inhabitants never.

Of Fruits

Chestnuts there are in divers places great store; some they eat raw, some they stamp and boil to make spoonmeat. With some, being sodden, they make such a manner of dough bread as they use of their beans before mentioned.

Walnuts. There are two kinds of walnuts, and of them infinite store; in many places, where are very great woods for many miles together, the third part of trees are walnut trees. The one kind is of the same taste and form, or little differing from ours of England, but that they are harder and thicker shelled. The other is greater and has a very ragged and hard shell, but the kernel great, very oily and sweet. Besides their eating of them after our ordinary manner, they break them with stones and crush them in mortars with water, to make a milk which they put into some sorts of their spoonmeat; also among their sodden wheat, peas, beans and pumpkins, which makes them have a far more pleasant taste.

Medlars, a kind of very good fruit; so called by us chiefly for these respects: first in that they are not good until they are rotten, then in that they open at the head as our medlars and are about the same bigness. Otherwise in taste and colour they are far different; for they are as red as cherries and very sweet. But whereas the cherry is sharp sweet, they are luscious sweet.

Mutaquesunnauk, a kind of pleasant fruit almost of the shape and bigness of English pears, but that they are of a perfect red colour as well within as without. They grow on a plant whose leaves are very thick, and full of prickles as sharp as needles. Some that have been in the Indies, where they have seen that kind of red dye of great price which is called cochineal, to grow, do describe its plant right like unto this of *Metaquesunnauk*. But whether it be the true cochineal, or a bastard or wild kind, it cannot yet be certified; seeing also, as I heard, cochineal is not of the fruit but found on the leaves of the plant: which leaves for such matter we have not so specially observed.

Grapes there are of two sorts, which I mentioned in the merchantable commodities.

Strawberries there are as good and as great as those which we have in our English gardens.

Mulberries, applecrabs, hurts or hurtleberries, such as we have in England.

Sacquenummener, a kind of berries almost like unto capers, but somewhat greater, which grow together in clusters upon a plant or herb that is found in shallow waters. Being boiled eight or nine hours according to their kind are very good meat and wholesome; otherwise if they be eaten they will make a man for the time frantic or extremely sick.

There is a kind of reed which bears a seed almost like unto our rye or wheat; and being boiled is good meat.

In our travels in some places we found wild peas like unto ours in England, but that they were less, which are also good meat.

Of a Kind of Fruit or Berry in Form of Acorns

There is a kind of berry or acorn of which there are five sorts that grow on several kinds of trees: the one is called *sagatemener*, the second *osamener*, the third *pummuckoner*. These kind of acorns they dry upon hurdles made of reeds, with fire underneath, almost after the manner as we dry malt in England. When they are to be used, they first water them until they are soft and then, being sodden, they make a good victual, either to eat so simply, or else being also crushed to make loaves or lumps of bread. These are also the three kinds of which I said the inhabitants make sweet oil.

Another sort is called *sapummener*, which being boiled or parched, does eat and taste like chestnuts. They sometimes also make bread of this sort.

The fifth sort is called *mangummenauk* and is the acorn of their kind of oak; which being dried after the manner of the first sorts and afterward watered, they boil them, and their servants or sometimes the chiefs themselves, either for variety or for want of bread, do eat them with their fish or flesh.

Of Beasts

Deer in some places there is great store. Near unto the sea coast they are of the ordinary bigness of ours in England, and some less; but further up into the country, where there is better food, they are greater. They differ from ours only in this, their tails are longer, and the snags of their horns look backward.

Conies. Those that we have seen and all that we can hear of are of a grey colour like unto hares. In some places there are such plenty that all the people of some towns make them mantles of the fur of the skins of those which they usually take.

Saquenuckot and *maquowoc*, two kinds of small beasts greater than the conies, which are very good meat. We never took any of them ourselves, but sometimes ate of such as the inhabitants had taken and brought unto us.

Squirrels, which are of a grey colour, we have taken and eaten.

Bears, which are of black colour. The bears of this country are good meat. The inhabitants in time of winter do take and eat many; so also sometimes did we. They are taken commonly in this sort. In some islands or places where they are, being hunted for, as soon as they have spial of a man, they run away. Being chased, they climb and get up the next tree they can; whence with arrows they are shot down stark dead, or with those wounds that they may after easily be killed. We sometimes shot them down with our calivers.

I have the names of eight-and-twenty several sorts of beasts, which I have heard of to be here and there dispersed in the country, especially in the mainland; of which there are only twelve kinds that we have yet discovered; of those that are good meat we know only them before mentioned. The inhabitants sometimes kill the lion [panther], and eat him; and we sometimes as they came to our hands of their wolves or wolvish dogs; which I have not set down for good meat, lest some would understand my judgement therein to be more simple than needs. Although I could allege the difference in taste of those kinds from ours, which by some of our company have experimented in both.

Of Fowl

Turkey cocks and turkey hens, stockdoves, partridges, cranes, herons, and in winter great store of swans and geese. Of all sorts of fowl I have the names in the country language of eighty-six; of which number, besides those that are named, we have taken, eaten, and have the pictures as they were there drawn, with the names by the inhabitants, of several strange sorts of water fowl eight, and seventeen kinds more of land fowl. We have seen and eaten many more, which for want of leisure there could not be pictured. After we are better furnished and stored upon further discovery with their strange beasts, fish, trees, plants, and herbs, they shall also be published.

There are also parrots, falcons, and merlin hawks.

Of Fish

For four months of the year, February, March, April and May, there are plenty of sturgeons. Also in the same months of herrings; some of the ordinary bigness of ours in England, but the most part far greater, of eighteen, twenty inches and some two foot in length and better. Both these kinds of fish in those months are most plentiful, and in best season; which we found to be most delicate and pleasant meat.

There are also trouts, porpoises, rays, breams, mullets, plaice, and very many other sorts of excellent good fish, which we have taken and eaten, whose names I know not but in the country language. We have the pictures of twelve sorts more, as they were drawn in the country, with their names.

The inhabitants take them in two ways. The one is by a kind of weir made of reeds, which in that country are very strong. The other way, which is more strange, is with poles made sharp at one end, by shooting them into the fish after the manner as Irishmen cast darts; either as they are rowing in their boats, or else as they are wading in the shallows for the purpose.

There are also in many places plenty of these kinds which follow:

Sea-crabs, such as we have in England.

Oysters, some very great, and some small, some round, and some of a long shape. They are found both in salt water and brackish; those that we had out of salt water are far better than the other, as in our country.

Also mussels, scallops, periwinkles and crayfish.

Seekanauk [king-crabs], a kind of crusty shell-fish, which is good meat, about a foot in breadth, having a crusty tail, many legs like a crab, and her eyes in her back. They are found in shallows of waters, and sometimes on the shore.

There are many turtles, both of land and sea kind, their backs and bellies are shelled very thick; their head, feet, and tail in appearance seem ugly, as though they were members of a serpent or venomous beasts. Notwithstanding, they are very good meat, as also their eggs. Some have been found of a yard in breadth and better.

Thus have I made relation of all sorts of victual that we fed upon for the time we were in Virginia, as also the inhabitants themselves, as far forth as I know and can remember, or that are specially worthy to be remembered.

The Third and last Part of such other things as are behoveful for those who shall plant and inhabit to know of, with a description of the nature and manners of the people of the country

Of Commodities for Building and other Necessary Uses

Those other things are such as concern building, and other mechanical necessary uses – as divers sorts of trees for house and ship-timber, and other uses else. Also lime, stone, and brick, lest being not mentioned some might have been doubted of, or by some that are malicious the contrary reported.

Oaks there are as fair, straight, tall, and as good timber as any can be, and also great store, and in some places very great.

Walnut trees very many; some have been seen excellent fair timber of four and five fathoms, and above eighty foot straight without bough.

Fir trees fit for masts of ships, some very tall and great.

Rakiock, a kind of trees so called that are sweet wood; of which the inhabitants that were near unto us do commonly make their boats or canoes of the form of troughs, only with the help of fire, hatchets of stone, and shells. We have known some so great, being made in that sort of one tree, that they have carried well twenty men at once, besides much baggage. The timber being great, tall, straight, soft, light, and yet tough enough, I think (besides other uses) to be fit also for masts of ships.

Cedar, a sweet wood good for ceilings, chests, boxes, bedsteads, lutes, virginals, and many things else. Some of our company, who have wandered in some places where I have not been, have made certain affirmation of cypress, which for such and other excellent uses is also a wood of price and no small estimation.

Maple, and also witch-hazel, whereof the inhabitants make their bows.

Holly, a necessary thing for the making of birdlime.

Willows, good for the making of weirs and traps to take fish after the English manner. The inhabitants use only reeds, which, because they are so strong as also flexible, do serve for that turn very well.

Beech and ash, good for cask-hoops, and if need require, plough work, as also for many things else.

Elm and Sassafras trees.

Ascopo, a kind of tree very like unto laurel; the bark is hot in taste and spicy. It is very like that tree which Monardes describes to be *Cassia Lignea* of the West Indies.

There are many other strange trees whose names I know not but in the Virginia language.

Not for stone, brick, and lime, thus it is. Near unto the sea coast where we dwelt, there are no kind of stones to be found (except a few small pebbles about four miles off), but such as have been brought from further out of the mainland. In some of our voyages we have seen divers hard ragged stones, great pebbles, and a kind of grey stone like marble, of which the inhabitants make their hatchets to cleave wood. We heard that a little further up into the country were of all sorts very many; although of quarries they are ignorant, neither have they use of any store whereupon they should have occasion to seek any. For if every household has one or two to crack nuts, grind shells, whet copper, and sometimes other stones for hatchets, they have enough. Neither use they any digging, but only for graves about three feet deep; and therefore no marvel that they know neither quarries, nor lime-stones, which both may be in places nearer than they know of.

Until there is discovery of sufficient store in some place or other convenient, the want of you who are and shall be the planters therein may be as well supplied by brick. For making whereof in divers places of the country there is clay both excellent and good, and plenty. Also by lime made of oyster shells, and of others burnt, after the manner they use in the Isles of Thanet and Sheppey, and in other places of England. Which kind of lime is well known to be as good as any other. Of oyster shells there is plenty enough. Besides other particular places where are abundance, there is one shallow sound along the coast, where for the space of many miles together in length and two or three miles in breadth, the ground is nothing else, being but half a foot or a foot under water for the most part.

Thus much can I say furthermore of stones, that about 120 miles from our fort near the water in the side of a hill, was found by a gentleman of our company a great vein of hard rag stones.

Of the Nature and Manners of the People

It rests I speak a word or two of the natural inhabitants, their natures and manners, leaving large discourse thereof until time more convenient hereafter. Now only so far forth as that you may know that they, in respect of troubling our inhabiting and planting, are not to be feared; but that they shall have cause both to fear and love us that shall inhabit with them.

They are a people clothed with loose mantles made of deer skins, and aprons of the same round about their middles, all else naked; of such a difference of statures only as we in England; having no edge tools or weapons of iron or steel to offend us with, neither know they how to make any. Those weapons that they have are only bows made of witch-hazel and arrows of reeds; flat-edged truncheons also of wood about a yard long. Neither have they anything to defend themselves but shields made of barks, and some armours made of sticks wickered together with thread.

Their towns are but small, and near the sea coast but few, some containing but ten or twelve houses; some twenty. The greatest that we have seen has been but of thirty houses. If they are walled, it is only done with barks of trees made fast to stakes, or else with poles fixed upright and close one by another.

Their houses are made of small poles, made fast at the tops in round form after the manner as is used in many arbours in our gardens of England; in most towns covered with barks, and in some with mats made of long rushes, from the tops of the houses down to the ground. The length of them is commonly double the breadth, in some places they are but twelve and sixteen yards long, and in others we have seen twenty-four.

In some places of the country, one only town belongs to the government of a *weroance* or chief lord; in others two or three, in some six, eight, and more. The greatest *weroance* that yet we had dealing with has but eighteen towns in his government, and able to make not above seven or eight hundred fighting men at the most. The language of every government is different from any other, and the further they are distant the greater is the difference.

Their manner of wars among themselves is either by sudden surprising one another, most commonly about the dawning of the day, or moonlight, or else by ambushes or some subtle devices. Set battles are very rare, except it falls out where there are many trees; where either part may have some hope of defence, after the delivery of every arrow, in leaping behind some or other.

If there fall out any wars between us and them, what their fight is likely to be, we having advantages against them so many ways – as by our discipline, our strange weapons and devices else, especially ordnance great and small – it may easily be imagined. By the experience we have had in some places the turning up of their heels in running away was their best defence.

In respect of us they are a people poor, and for want of

skill and judgement in the knowledge and use of our things, do esteem our trifles before things of greater value. Notwithstanding in their own manner (considering the want of such means as we have), they seem very ingenious. For although they have no such tools, nor any such crafts, sciences and arts as we, yet in those things they do, they show excellence of wit. By how much they shall find our knowledges and crafts to exceed theirs in perfection, and speed for doing or execution, by so much the more is it probable that they should desire our friendship and love, and have the greater respect for pleasing and obeying us. Whereby may be hoped, if means of good government are used that they may in short time be brought to civility and the embracing of true religion.

Some religion they have already, which although it is far from the truth, yet being as it is, there is hope it may be the easier and sooner reformed. They believe that there are many gods, which they call mantoac, but of different sorts and degrees, one only chief and great God, which has been from all eternity. Who, as they affirm, when he purposed to make the world, made first other gods of a principal order to be as means and instruments to be used in the creation and government to follow; after the sun, moon, and stars as petty gods, and the instruments of the other order more principal. First (they say) were made waters, out of which by the gods was made all diversity of creatures that are visible or invisible.

For mankind they say a woman was made first, who by the working of one of the gods, conceived and brought forth children. And in such sort they say they had their beginning. But how many years or ages have passed since they say they can make no relation, having no letters nor other such means as we to keep records of the particularities of times past, but only tradition from father to son.

They think that all the gods are of human shape, and therefore they represent them by images in the forms of men, which they call *kewasowok*, one alone is called *kewas*. Them they place in houses appropriate or temples, which they call *machicomuck*, where they worship, pray, sing, and make many times offering unto them. In some *machicomuck* we have seen but one *kewas*, in some two, and in others three. The common sort think them to be also gods.

They believe also the immortality of the soul – that after this life as soon as the soul is departed from the body, according to the works it has done, it is either carried to heaven the habitacle of gods, there to enjoy perpetual bliss and happiness; or else to a great pit or hole. This they think to be in the farthest parts of their part of the world toward the sunset, there to burn continually: the place they call Popogusso.

For the confirmation of this opinion they told me two stories of two men that had been lately dead and revived again. The one happened but few years before our coming into the country – of a wicked man, who having been dead and buried, the next day the earth of the grave being seen to move, was taken up again. He made declaration where his soul had been, that is to say, very near entering into Popogusso, had not one of the gods saved him, and gave him leave to return and teach his friends what they should do to avoid that terrible place of torment.

The other happened in the same year we were there, but in a town that was sixty miles from us. It was told me for strange news that one being dead, buried, and taken up again as the first, showed that although his body had lain dead in the grave, yet his soul was alive. He had travelled far in a long broad way on both sides whereof grew most delicate and pleasant trees, bearing more rare and excellent fruits than ever he had seen before, or was able to express. He at length came to most brave and fair houses, near which he met his father that had been dead before, who gave him great charge to go back and show his friends what good they were to do to enjoy the pleasures of that place. When he had done this he should after come again.

What subtlety soever is in the *weroances* and priests, this opinion works so much in many of the common and simple sort of people, that it makes them have great respect to their governors. And also great care what they do, to avoid torment after death, and to enjoy bliss. Notwithstanding there is punishment ordained for malefactors, as stealers, whoremongers, and other sorts of wicked doers; some punished with death, some with forfeitures, some with beating, according to the greatness of the facts.

This is the sum of their religion, which I learned by having special familiarity with some of their priests. Wherein they were not so sure grounded nor gave such credit to their traditions and stories, but through conversing with us they were brought into great doubts of their own and no small admiration of ours. With earnest desire in many to learn more than we had means for want of perfect utterance in their language to express.

Most things they saw with us, as mathematical instruments, sea compasses, the virtue of the loadstone in drawing iron, a perspective glass whereby was shown many sights, burning glasses, wild fireworks, guns, hooks, writing and reading, spring-clocks that seem to go of themselves and many other things that we had were so strange unto them. They so far exceeded their capacities to comprehend the reason and means how they should be made and done that they thought they were rather the works of gods than of men, or at the least they had been given and taught us by the gods.

This made many of them to have such opinion of us as that, if they knew not the truth of God and religion already, it was rather to be had from us whom God so specially loved, than from a people that were so simple as they found themselves to be in comparison with us. Whereupon greater credit was given unto that we spoke of, concerning such matters.

Many times and in every town where I came, according as I was able, I made declaration of the contents of the Bible; that therein was set forth the true and only God and his mighty works, that therein was contained the true doctrine of salvation through Christ, with many particularities of miracles and chief points of religion. Although I told them the book materially was not any such virtue as they did conceive, but only the doctrine therein contained, yet would many be glad to touch it, to embrace it, to kiss it, to hold it to their breasts and heads, and stroke over all their body with it, to show their hungry desire of that knowledge which was spoken of.

The *weroance* with whom we dwelt, called Wingina, and many of his people would be glad many times to be with us at our prayers, and many times call upon us in his own town as also in others whither he sometimes accompanied us, to pray and sing psalms. Hoping thereby to be partaker of the same effects which we by that means also expected.

Twice this *weroance* was so grievously sick that he was likely to die. As he lay languishing, doubting of any help by his own priests, and thinking he was in such danger for offending us and thereby our God, he sent for some of us to pray and be a means to our God that it would please him either that he might live, or after death dwell with him in bliss. So likewise were the requests of many others in the like case.

On a time also when their corn began to wither by reason of a drought which happened extraordinarily, fearing that it had come to pass by reason that in some thing they had displeased us, many would desire us to pray to our God of England, that he would preserve their corn. Promising that when it was ripe we also should be partakers of the fruit.

There could at no time happen any strange sickness, losses, hurts, or any other cross unto them, but that they would impute to us the cause or means thereof, for offending or not pleasing us. One other rare and strange accident, leaving others, will I mention before I end, which moved the whole country that either knew or heard of us to have us in wonder.

There was no town where we had any subtle device practised against us, we leaving it unpunished or not revenged (because we sought by all means possible to win them by gentleness) but that, within a few days after our departure, the people began to die very fast. Many in short space, in some towns about twenty, in some forty, and in one a hundred and twenty: which in truth was very many in respect of their numbers. This happened in no place that we could learn, but where we had been where they used some practice against us, and after such time. The disease also was so strange that they neither knew what it was, nor how to cure it. The like by report of the oldest men in the country never happened before, time out of mind. A thing specially observed by us, as also by the natural inhabitants themselves.

Insomuch that when some of the inhabitants who were our friends, and especially the *weroance* Wingina, had observed such effects in four or five towns to follow their wicked practices, they were persuaded that it was the work of our God through our means: that we by him might kill and slay whom we would without weapons, and not come near them. When they had understanding that any of their enemies had abused us in our journeys, hearing that we had wrought no revenge with our weapons, they did entreat us that we would be a means to our God that they as others that had dealt ill with us might in like sort die. Alleging how much it would be for our credit and profit, as also theirs, and hoping furthermore that we would do so much at their request in respect of the friendship we professed them.

Whose entreaties although we showed that they were ungodly, affirming that our God would not subject himself to any such prayers and requests of men; indeed all things have been and were to be done according to his good pleasure as he had ordained. We to show ourselves his true servants ought rather to make petition for the contrary, that they with them might live together with us, be made partakers of his truth, and serve him in righteousness. Notwithstanding we refer that, as all other things, to be done according to his divine will and pleasure, and as by his wisdom he had ordained to be best.

Yet because the effect fell out so shortly after according to their desires, they thought nevertheless it came to pass by our means, and that we did but dissemble the matter. They therefore came unto us to give us thanks in their manner that, although we satisfied them not in promise, yet in deeds and effect we had fulfilled their desires.

This marvellous accident in all the country wrought so strange opinions of us that some people could not tell whether to think us gods or men. The rather because, all the space of their sickness, there was no man of ours known to die or that was specially sick. They noted also that we had no women among us, neither that we did care for any of theirs.

Some therefore were of opinion that we were not born of women, and therefore not mortal; but that we were men of an old generation many years past, then risen again to immortality.

Some would likewise seem to prophesy that there were more of our generation yet to come to kill theirs and take their places, as some thought the purpose was by that which was already done. Those that were immediately to come after us they imagined to be in the air, yet invisible and without bodies; and that they, by our entreaty and for the love of us, did make the people to die in that sort as they did by shooting invisible bullets into them.

To confirm this opinion their physicians (to excuse their ignorance in curing the disease) would not be ashamed to say but earnestly make the simple people believe, that the strings of blood they sucked out of the sick bodies were the strings wherewith the invisible bullets were tied and cast. Some also thought that we shot them ourselves out of our pieces from the place where we dwelt, and killed the people in any town that had offended us, as we listed, how far distant from us soever it was. Others said that it was the special work of God for our sakes, as we ourselves have cause in some sort to think no less, whatsoever some may imagine to the contrary. Specially some astrologers, knowing of the eclipse of the sun which we saw the same year before in our voyage thitherward, which unto them appeared very terrible. And also of a comet which began to appear but a few days before the beginning of the said sickness. But to exclude them from being the special causes of so special an accident, there are further reasons than I think fit at this present to be alleged. These their opinions I have set down the more at large that it may appear unto you that there is good hope they may be brought through discreet dealing and government to the embracing of the truth, and consequently to honour, obey, fear and love us.

Some of our company towards the end of the year showed themselves too fierce in slaying some of the people in some towns, upon causes that on our part might easily enough have been borne with. Notwithstanding, because it was on their part justly deserved, the alteration of their opinions for the most part concerning us is the less to be doubted. And whatsoever else they may be, by carefulness of ourselves need nothing at all to be feared.

The Conclusion

Now I have (as I hope) made relation not of so few and small things but that the country (of men that are impartial and well disposed) may be sufficiently liked. If there were no more known than I have mentioned, which doubtless and in great reason is nothing to that which remains to be discovered, neither the soil, nor commodities. As we have reason so to gather by the difference we found in our travels, although all that I have before spoken of has been discovered and experienced not far from the sea coast, where was our abode and most of our travelling. Sometimes as we made our journeys further into the mainland, we found the soil to be fatter, the trees greater and to grow thinner, the ground more firm and deeper mould, more and larger champaigns, finer grass, and as good as ever we saw any in England. In some places rocky and far more high and hilly ground, more plenty of their fruits, more abundance of beasts, the more inhabited with people, and of greater policy and larger dominions were greater towns and houses.

Why may we not then look for in good hope from the inner parts of more and greater plenty, as well of other things, as of those which we have already discovered? Unto the Spaniards happened the like in discovering the mainland from the West Indies. The mainland also of Virginia, extending some ways so many hundreds of leagues, as otherwise than by the relation of the inhabitants we have most certain knowledge of, where yet no Christian prince has any possession or dealing, cannot but yield many kinds of excellent commodities which we in our discovery have not yet seen.

What hope there is else to be gathered of the nature of the climate, being answerable to the islands of Japan, the land of China, Persia, Jewry, and islands of Cyprus and Crete, the south parts of Greece, Italy and Spain, and of many other notable and famous countries, I leave to your own consideration.

Whereby also the excellent temperature of the air there at all seasons, much warmer than in England, and never so vehemently hot as sometimes is under and between the

Tropics, or near them, cannot be known unto you without further relation.

For the wholesomeness thereof I need to say but thus much: for all the want of provision, as first of English victual, excepting for twenty days we lived only by drinking water, and by the victual of the country. Some sorts were very strange unto us, and might have been thought to have altered our temperatures in such sort as to have brought us into some grievous and dangerous diseases. Secondly, the want of English means for the taking of beasts, fish and fowl. By the help only of the inhabitants and their means these could not be so suddenly and easily provided for us, nor in so great number and quantities, nor of that choice as otherwise might have been to our better satisfaction. Some want also we had of clothes.

Furthermore in all our travels, which were most often in the time of winter, our lodging was in the open air upon the ground. Yet for all this there were but four of our whole company (being a hundred and eight) that died all the year, and that but at the latter end thereof and upon none of the aforesaid causes. For all four, especially three, were feeble, weak, and sickly persons before ever they came thither; those that knew them much marvelled that they lived so long or had adventured to travel.

Seeing therefore the air there is so temperate and wholesome, the soil so fertile and yielding such commodities as I have before mentioned, the voyage also thither to and fro being sufficiently experienced to be performed twice a year with ease, and at any season thereof; and the dealing of Sir Walter Raleigh so liberal in large giving and granting land there, as is already known, with many helps and furtherances else (the least that he has granted has been five hundred acres to a man only for the adventure of his person) – I hope there remains no cause whereby the action should be misliked.

If those who shall thither travail to inhabit and plant are but reasonably provided for the first year, as those are who were transported the last and, being there, do use but that diligence and care that is requisite – there is no doubt but for the time following they may have victuals that are excellent good and plenty enough; some more English sorts of cattle also hereafter, as some have been before and are there yet remaining, may and shall be (God willing) thither transported. So likewise our kind of fruits, roots, and herbs may be there planted and sowed, as some have been already, and prove well. In short time also they may raise so much of those sorts of commodities which I have spoken of as shall both enrich themselves, as also others that shall deal with them.

This is all the fruit of our labours that I have thought necessary to advertise you of at this present. What else concerns the nature and manners of the inhabitants of Virginia, the number with the particularities of the voyages thither made; of the actions of such as have been by Sir Walter Raleigh therein and there employed, many worthy to be remembered, as of the first discoverers of the country, of our general for the time Sir Richard Grenville, and after his departure of our governor there, master Ralph Lane, with divers others directed and employed under their government; of the captains and masters of the voyages made since for transportation; of the governor and assistants of those already transported, as of many persons, events, and things else – I have ready in a discourse by itself in manner of a chronicle, according to the course of times. This, when time shall be thought convenient, shall be also published.

Thus referring my relation to your favourable constructions, expecting good success of the action, from him who is to be acknowledged the author and governor, not only of this but of all things else, I take my leave of you, this month of February 1587.

12

THE THIRD VIRGINIA VOYAGE, 1586

The Third Voyage made by a ship sent in the year 1586, to the relief of the Colony planted in Virginia, at the sole charges of Sir Walter Raleigh.

In the year of our Lord 1586 Sir Walter Raleigh at his own charge prepared a ship of an hundred tons, freighted with all manner of things in most plentiful manner, for the supply and relief of his Colony then remaining in Virginia. But before they set sail from England it was after Easter, so that our Colony half despaired of the coming of any supply. Wherefore every man prepared for himself, determining resolutely to spend the residue of their lifetime in that country. And for the better performance of this their determination, they sowed, planted, and set such things as were necessary for their relief in so plentiful a manner as might have sufficed them two years without any further labour. Thus trusting to their own harvest, they passed the summer till the tenth of June; at which time their corn which they had sowed was within one fortnight of reaping.

But then it happened that Sir Francis Drake in his prosperous return from the sacking of San Domingo, Cartagena, and Saint Augustine, determined in his way homeward to visit his countrymen the English Colony then remaining in Virginia. So passing along the coasts of Florida, he fell with the parts where our English Colony inhabited. Having espied some of that company, there he anchored and went on land; where he conferred with them of their state and welfare, and how things had passed with them. They answered him that they lived all, but hitherto in some scarcity; and as yet could hear of no supply out of England. Therefore they requested him that he would leave with them some two or three ships, that if in some reasonable time they heard not out of England, they might then return themselves. Which he agreed to.

While some were then writing their letters to send into England, and some others making reports of the accidents of their travels each to other, some on land, some on board, a great storm arose, and drove the most of their fleet from their anchors to sea, in which ships were the chiefest of the English Colony. The rest on land perceiving this hasted to those three sails which were appointed to be left there. And for fear they should be left behind they left all things confusedly, as if they had been chased from thence by a mighty army. And no doubt so they were; for the hand of God came upon them for the cruelty and outrages committed by some of them against the native inhabitants of that country.

Immediately after the departing of our English Colony out of this paradise of the world, the ship above mentioned sent and set forth at the charges of Sir Walter Raleigh and his direction, arrived at Hatorask; which after some time spent in seeking our Colony up in the country, and not finding them, returned with all the aforesaid provision into England.

About fourteen or fifteen days after the departure of the ship, Sir Richard Grenville, general of Virginia, accompanied with three ships well appointed for the same voyage, arrived there. Not finding the aforesaid ship according to his expectation, nor hearing any news of our English Colony there left by him anno 1585, himself travelled up into divers places of the country, to see if he could hear any news of the Colony left under the charge of Master Lane his deputy, as also to discover some places of the country. But after some time spent therein, not hearing any news of them, and finding the places which they inhabited desolate, yet unwilling to lose the possession of the country which Englishmen had so long held, after good deliberation, he determined to leave some men behind to retain possession of the country. Whereupon he landed fifteen men in the isle of Roanoke, furnished plentifully with all manner of provision for two years, and so departed for England.

Not long after he fell with the isles of Azores, on some of which islands he landed and spoiled the towns of all such things as were worth carriage, where also he took divers Spaniards. With these and many other exploits done by him in this voyage, as well outward as homeward, he returned unto England.

13

THE LOST (SECOND) COLONY, 1587

*The Fourth Voyage made to Virginia with three ships, in the year 1587.
Wherein was transported the Second Colony.*

In the year of our Lord 1587 Sir Walter Raleigh, intending to
persevere in the planting of his country of Virginia, prepared
a new Colony of one hundred and fifty men to be sent
thither, under the charge of John White, whom he appointed
Governor. He also appointed unto him twelve assistants, unto
whom he gave a charter, and incorporated them by the name
of Governor and Assistants of the City of Raleigh in Virginia.

April: Our fleet being in number three sail, viz, the Admiral
a ship of 120 tons, a fly-boat, and a pinnace, departed the
six-and-twentieth of April from Portsmouth, and the same
day came to anchor at Cowes in the Isle of Wight, where we
stayed eight days.

May: The fifth of May, at nine of the clock at night we
came to Plymouth, where we remained the space of two days.
The eighth we weighed anchor at Plymouth, and departed
thence for Virginia. The sixteenth Simon Ferdinandez, master
of our Admiral, lewdly forsook our fly-boat, leaving her
distressed in the bay of Portugal.

June: the nineteenth we fell with Dominica, and the same
evening we sailed between it, and Guadalupe; the twenty-first
the fly-boat also fell with Dominica. The twenty-second we
came to anchor at an island called Santa Cruz, where all the
planters were set on land, staying there till the twenty-fifth
of the same month. At our first landing on this island some
of our women and men, by eating a small fruit like green
apples, were fearfully troubled with a sudden burning in their

mouths, and swelling of their tongues so big that some of them could not speak. Also a child, by sucking one of those women's breasts, had his mouth set on such a burning that it was strange to see how the infant was tormented for the time. But after twenty-four hours it wore away of itself.

Also the first night of our being on this island, we took five great turtles, some of them of such bigness that sixteen of our strongest men were tired with carrying one of them but from the seaside to our cabins. In this island we found no watering place but a standing pond, the water whereof was so evil that many of our company fell sick with drinking thereof. And as many as did but wash their faces with that water, in the morning before the sun had drawn away the corruption, their faces did so burn and swell that their eyes were shut up and could not see in five or six days, or longer.

The second day of our abode there, we sent forth some of our men to search the island for fresh water, three one way, and two another way. The governor also, with six others, went up to the top of an high hill to view the island, but could perceive no sign of any men or beasts, nor any goodness, but parrots, and trees of *guaiacum*. Returning back to our cabins another way, he found in the descent of a hill certain pot shards of savage making, made of the earth of that island. Whereupon it was judged that this island was inhabited with savages, though Fernandez had told us for certain the contrary. The same day at night the rest of our company very late returned to the governor. The one company affirmed that they had seen in a valley eleven savages and divers houses half a mile distant from the top of the hill where they stayed. The other company had found running out of a high rock a very fair spring of water, whereof they brought three bottles to the company; for before that time, we drank the stinking water of the pond.

The same second day at night Captain Stafford with the pinnace departed from our fleet, riding at Santa Cruz, to an island, called Beake, lying near St John, being so directed by Ferdinandez, who assured him he should there find great plenty of sheep. The next day at night our planters left Santa Cruz and came all aboard; the next morning, being the twenty-fifth of June, we weighed anchor and departed from

Santa Cruz. The seven-and-twentieth we came to anchor at Cottea, where we found the pinnace riding at our coming. The twenty-eighth we weighed anchor at Cottea, and presently came to anchor at St John's in Mosquito Bay. Here we spent three days unprofitably in taking in fresh water, spending in the meantime more beer than the quantity of the water came unto.

July: The first day we weighed anchor at Mosquito Bay – where were left behind two Irishmen of our company – bearing along the coast of St John's till evening, at which time we fell with Rosse Bay. At this place Ferdinandez had promised we should take in salt, and had caused us to provide as many sacks for that purpose as we could. The governor, who understood there was a town in the bottom of the bay, not far from the salt hills, appointed thirty shot, ten pikes, and ten shields, to man the pinnace and to go on land for salt. Ferdinandez perceiving them in a readiness sent to the governor, using great persuasions with him not to take in salt there, saying that he knew not well whether the same were the place or not. Also, that if the pinnace went into the bay, she could not without great danger come back till the next day at night. If in the meantime any storm should rise the Admiral were in danger to be cast away. While he was thus persuading he caused the lead to be cast, and having craftily brought the ship in three fathom and a half water, he suddenly began to swear and tear God in pieces, dissembling great danger, crying to him at the helm, 'Bear up hard, bear up hard.' So we went off, and were disappointed of our salt by his means.

The next day sailing along the west end of St John, the governor determined to go on land in St German's Bay, to gather young plants of oranges, pines, mameas, and bananas to set at Virginia. These we knew might easily be had, for they grow near the shore, and the places where they grew well known to the governor and some of the planters. But our Simon denied it, saying: he would come to an anchor at Hispaniola and there land the governor, and some others of the assistants, with the pinnace: to see if he could speak with his friend Alençon, of whom he hoped to be furnished both of cattle and all such things as we would have taken in at St

John. But he meant nothing less, as it plainly did appear to us afterwards.

The next day after, being the third of July, we saw Hispaniola, and bore with the coast all that day, looking still when the pinnace should be prepared to go for the place where Ferdinandez' friend Alençon was. But that day passed and we saw no preparation for landing in Hispaniola. The fourth of July, sailing along the coast of Hispaniola until the next day at noon, and no preparation yet seen for staying there, we having knowledge that we were past the place where Alençon dwelt and were come with Isabella. Hereupon Ferdinandez was asked by the governor whether he meant to speak with Alençon for the taking in of cattle and other things, according to his promise, or not. He answered that he was now past the place, and that Sir Walter Raleigh told him the French ambassador certified that the king of Spain had sent for Alençon in Spain. Wherefore he thought him dead, and that it was to no purpose to touch there in any place at this voyage.

The next day we left sight of Hispaniola, and haled off for Virginia, about four of the clock in the afternoon.

The sixth of July we came to the island Caicos, wherein Ferdinandez said were two salt ponds, assuring us if they were dry, we might find salt to shift with until the next supply. But it proved as true as finding of sheep at Beake. In this island, while Ferdinandez solaced himself ashore with one of the company in part of the island, others spent the latter part of that day in other parts of the island; some to seek the salt ponds, some fowling, some hunting swans, whereof we caught many. The next day early in the morning we weighed anchor, leaving Caicos with good hope that the first land that we saw next should be Virginia.

About the sixteenth of July we fell with the mainland of Virginia, which Simon Ferdinandez took to be the island of Croatoan, where we came to anchor, and rode there two or three days. But finding himself deceived, he weighed and bore along the coast. In the night, had not captain Stafford been more careful in looking out than our Simon Ferdinandez, we had been all cast away upon the breach called the Cape of Fear. For we were come within two cables' length upon it, such was the carelessness and ignorance of our master.

The two-and-twentieth of July we arrived safe at Hatorask, where our ship and pinnace anchored. The governor went aboard the pinnace, accompanied with forty of his best men, intending to pass up to Roanoke forthwith. Hoping there to find those fifteen Englishmen, whom Sir Richard Grenville had left there the year before, with whom he meant to have conference concerning the state of the country and savages. Meaning after he had so done to return again to the fleet, and pass along the coast to the bay of Chesapeake, where we intended to make our seat and fort, according to the charge given us among other directions in writing, under the hand of Sir Walter Raleigh.

But as soon as we were put with our pinnace from the ship, a gentleman by the means of Ferdinandez, who was appointed to return to England, called to the sailors in the pinnace, charging them not to bring any of the planters back again, but to leave them in the island, except the governor and two or three such as he approved. Saying that the summer was far spent, wherefore he would land all the planters in no other place. Unto this were all the sailors, both in the pinnace and ship, persuaded by the master. Wherefore it booted not the governor to contend with them, but passed to Roanoke and at sunset went on land on the island, in the place where our fifteen men were left. But we found none of them, nor any sign that they had been there, saving only we found the bones of one of those fifteen, whom the savages had slain long before.

The three-and-twentieth of July the governor, with divers of his company, walked to the north end of the island. Here master Ralph Lane had his fort, with sundry necessary and decent dwelling houses, made by his men the year before, where we hoped to find some signs or certain knowledge of our fifteen men. When we came thither we found the fort razed down, but all the houses standing unhurt; saving that the nether rooms of them, and also of the fort, were over-grown with melons of divers sorts, and deer within them, feeding on those melons. So we returned to our company, without hope of ever seeing any of the fifteen men living.

The same day order was given that every man should be employed for the repairing of those houses which we found standing, and also to make other new cottages for such as should need.

The twenty-fifth our flyboat and the rest of our planters arrived all safe at Hatorask, to the great joy and comfort of the whole company. But the master of our Admiral, Ferdinandez, grieved greatly at their safe coming. For he purposely left them in the bay of Portugal, and stole away from them in the night, hoping that the master thereof, Edward Spicer, for that he never had been in Virginia, would hardly find the place. Or else being left in so dangerous a place as that was, by means of so many men of war as at that time were abroad, they should surely be taken or slain. But God disappointed his wicked intentions.

The eight-and-twentieth, George Howe, one of our twelve assistants was slain by divers savages, who were come over to Roanoke, either of purpose to espy our company and what number we were, or else to hunt deer, whereof were many in the island. These savages being secretly hidden among high reeds, where oftentimes they find the deer asleep and so kill them, espied our man wading in the water alone almost naked, without any weapon, save only a small forked stick, catching crabs therewith. He being strayed two miles from his company, they shot at him in the water, where they gave him sixteen wounds with their arrows. After they had slain him with their wooden swords, they beat his head in pieces, and fled over the water to the mainland.

On the thirtieth of July master Stafford and twenty of our men passed by water to the island of Croatoan, with Manteo. He had his mother and many of his kindred dwelling in that island, of whom we hoped to understand some news of our fifteen men, but especially to learn the disposition of the people of the country towards us, and to renew our old friendship with them. At our first landing they seemed as though they would fight with us; but perceiving us begin to march with our shot towards them, they turned their backs and fled. Then Manteo their countryman called to them in their own language. As soon as they heard him they returned, and threw away bows and arrows, and some of them came unto us, embracing and entertaining us friendly, desiring us not to gather or spill any of their corn, for that they had but little. We answered them that neither their corn nor any other thing of theirs should be diminished by any of us. Our coming was only to renew the old love that was between us and them at the first, and to live with them as brethren and friends: which answer seemed to please them well. They requested us to walk up to their town, who there feasted us after their manner, and desired us earnestly that there might be some token or badge given them of us, whereby we might know them to be our friends when we met them anywhere out of the town or island. They told us further that for want of some such badge divers of them were hurt the year before, being found out of the island by master Lane's company. Whereof they showed us one, who at that very instant lay lame, and had lain of that hurt ever since. But they said they knew our men mistook them, and hurt them instead of Wingina's men, wherefore they held us excused.

August: The next day we had conference further with them, concerning the people of Secotan, Aquascogoc, and Pomeiok; willing them of Croatoan to certify the people of those towns that, if they would accept our friendship, we would willingly receive them again, and that all unfriendly dealings past on both parts should be utterly forgiven and forgotten. To this the chief men of Croatoan answered that they would gladly do the best they could, and within seven days bring the *weroances* and chief governors of those towns with them to our governor at Roanoke, or their answer.

We also understood of the men of Croatoan that our man, master Howe, was slain by the remnant of Wingina's men dwelling then at Dasamonquepeio, with whom Wanchese kept company. Also we understood by them of Croatoan how that the fifteen Englishmen left at Roanoke the year before by Sir Richard Grenville were suddenly set upon by thirty of the men of Secotan, Aquascogoc, and Dasamonquepeio, in manner following. They conveyed themselves secretly behind the trees, near the houses where our men carelessly lived. Having perceived that of those fifteen they could see but eleven only, two of those savages appeared to the eleven Englishmen, calling to them by friendly signs that but two of their chiefest men should come unarmed to speak with those two savages, who seemed also to be unarmed.

Wherefore two of the chiefest of our Englishmen went gladly to them. But while one of those savages traitorously embraced one of our men, the other with his sword of wood, which he had secretly hidden under his mantle, struck him on the head and slew him. Immediately the other eight-and-twenty savages showed themselves. The other Englishman perceiving this fled to his company; whom the savages pursued with their bows and arrows so fast that the Englishmen were forced to take the house, wherein all their victual and weapons were. But the savages forthwith set the same on fire. By means whereof our men were forced to take up such weapons as came first to hand, and without order to run forth among the savages, with whom they skirmished above an hour.

In this skirmish another of our men was shot into the mouth with an arrow, whereof he died. Also one of the savages was shot into the side by one of our men with a wild fire arrow, whereof he died presently. The place where they fought was of great advantage to the savages by means of the thick trees, behind which the savages through their nimbleness defended themselves. They so offended our men with their arrows that our men, some of them hurt, retired fighting to the waterside, where their boat lay; with which they fled towards Hatorask. By that time they had rowed but a quarter of a mile, they espied their four fellows coming from a creek thereby, where they had been to fetch oysters. These four they received into their boat, leaving Roanoke and landed on a little island on the right hand of our entrance into the harbour of Hatorask, where they remained awhile, but afterward departed, whither as yet we know not. Having now sufficiently dispatched our business at Croatoan, the same day we departed friendly, taking our leave, and came aboard the fleet at Hatorask.

The eighth of August, the governor having long expected the coming of the *weroances* of Pomeiok, Aquascogoc, Secotan, and Dasamonquepeio – seeing that the seven days were past within which they promised to come in, or to send their answers by the men of Croatoan, and no tidings of them heard – being certainly also informed that the remnant of Wingina's men were they who had slain George Howe and were also at the driving of our eleven Englishmen from Roanoke, he thought to defer the revenge thereof no longer. Wherefore about midnight he passed over the water, accompanied with captain Stafford and twenty-four men, whereof Manteo was one, whom we took with us to be our guide to the place where those savages dwelt: where he behaved himself toward us as a most faithful Englishman.

The next day, being the ninth of August, in the morning so early that it was yet dark, we landed near the dwelling place of our enemies and very secretly conveyed ourselves through the woods to that side where we had their houses between us and the water. Having spied their fire and some sitting about it, we at once set on them. The miserable souls amazed fled into a place of thick reeds growing fast by, where our men perceiving them shot one of them through the body with a bullet. Therewith we entered the reeds, among which we hoped to acquit their evil doing towards us. But we were deceived, for those savages were our friends, and were come from Croatoan to gather the corn and fruit of that place. Because they understood our enemies were fled immediately after they had slain George Howe, and for haste had left all their corn, tobacco, and pumpkins standing in such sort that all had been devoured of the birds and deer, if it had not been gathered in time. But they had like to have paid dearly for it; for it was so dark that, they being naked and their men and women apparelled all so like others, we knew not but that they were all men. If that one of them who was a *weroance*'s wife had not had a child at her back, she had been slain instead of a man. As hap was, another savage knew master Stafford and ran to him, calling him by his name, whereby he was saved.

Finding ourselves thus disappointed of our purpose, we gathered all the corn, peas, pumpkins, and tobacco that we found ripe, leaving the rest unspoiled, and took Menatonon's wife with the young child and the other savages with us over the water to Roanoke. Although the mistaking of these savages somewhat grieved Manteo, yet he imputed their harm to their own folly; saying to them that, if their *weroances* had kept their promise in coming to the governor at the day appointed, they had not known that mischance. The thirteenth of August our savage Manteo, by the commandment of Sir Walter Raleigh, was christened in Roanoke and called lord thereof and of Dasamonquepeio, in reward of his faithful service.

The eighteenth Eleanor, daughter to the governor and wife to Ananias Dare, one of the assistants, was delivered of a daughter in Roanoke and the same was christened there the Sunday following. And because this child was the first Christian born in Virginia, she was named Virginia. By this time our ships had unladen the goods and victuals of the planters, and begun to take in wood, and fresh water, and to new calk and trim them for England. The planters also prepared their letters and tokens to send back into England. Our two ships, the *Lion* and the flyboat almost ready to depart, the twenty-first of August, there arose such a tempest at northeast, that our Admiral then riding out of the harbour was forced to cut his cables and put to sea. Where he lay beating off and on six days before he could come to us again; so that we feared he had been cast away, and the rather for that at the time the most and best of their sailors were left on land.

At this time some controversies arose between the governor and assistants, about choosing two out of the twelve assistants, who should go back as factors for the company into England. For every one of them refused save only one, whom all other thought not sufficient. At length by much persuading of the governor, Christopher Cooper only agreed to go for England; but the next day, through the persuasion of divers of his familiar friends, he changed his mind. So that now the matter stood as at the first.

The next day, the twenty-second of August, the whole company both of the assistants and planters came to the governor, and with one voice requested him to return himself into England, for the better and sooner obtaining of supplies and other necessaries for them. But he refused it, and alleged many sufficient causes why he would not. One was that he could not so suddenly return again without his great discredit, leaving the action and so many whom he partly had procured through his persuasions to leave their native country and undertake that voyage. Some enemies to him and the action would not spare to slander falsely both him and the action, by saying he went to Virginia but politicly, and to no other end but to lead so many into a country in which he never meant to stay himself, and there to leave them behind him. Also, seeing they intended to remove 50 miles further up into the mainland, he being then absent, his stuff and goods might be spoiled and most of them pilfered away in the carriage. At his return he should be either forced to provide himself of all such things again, or else at his coming again to Virginia find himself utterly unfurnished. Whereof already he had found some proof, being but once from them but three days. Wherefore he concluded that he would not go himself.

The next day not only the assistants but divers others began to renew their requests to the governor to return to England for the supply of all such things as there were to be done; promising to make him their bond under all their hands and seals for the safe preserving of all his goods for him at his return to Virginia. This bond they forthwith made and delivered into his hands. The copy of the testimony I thought good to set down.

May it please you, her Majesty's subjects of England, we your friends and countrymen, the planters in Virginia, have most earnestly entreated, and incessantly requested John White, governor of the planters in Virginia, to pass into England for the better and more assured help and setting forward of supplies . . . he not once but often refusing it, for our sakes and for the honour and maintenance of the action, has at last, though much against his will, through our importunacy, yielded to leave his government and all his goods among us, and himself in all our behalfs to pass into England, the twenty-fifth of August 1587.

The governor, being through their extreme entreating constrained to return to England, having then but half a day's respite to prepare himself, departed from Roanoke the seven-and-twentieth of August in the morning. The same day about midnight he came aboard the flyboat, which already had weighed anchor, and rode without the bar, the Admiral riding by them, which but the same morning was newly come thither again. The same day both the ships weighed anchor, and set sail for England. At this weighing their anchors twelve of the men in the flyboat was thrown from the capstan, which came so fast about upon them that two bars thereof struck and hurt most of them so sore that some never recovered it. Nevertheless they essayed again to weigh their anchor, but being so weakened with the first fling, they were not able to weigh it, but were thrown down and hurt the second time. Having in all but fifteen men aboard, and most of them by this unfortunate beginning so bruised and hurt, they were forced to cut their cable, and lose their anchor. Nevertheless, they kept company with the Admiral, until the seventeenth of September, at which time we fell with Corvo, and saw Flores.

September the eighteenth, of all our fifteen men in the flyboat there remained but five able to stand to their labour. The Admiral meant not to make any haste for England, but to linger about the island of Tercera for prizes. So the flyboat departed for England with letters, where we hoped by the help of God to arrive shortly. But by that time we had continued our course homeward about twenty days, having had sometimes scarce and variable winds, our fresh water also by leaking almost consumed, there arose a storm at northeast. For six days it ceased not to blow so exceeding that we were driven further in those six days that we could recover in thirteen days. In which time others of our sailors began to fall very sick and two of them died. The weather also continued so close that our master sometimes in four days together could see neither sun nor star, and all the beverage we could make, with stinking water, dregs of beer, and lees of wine was but three gallons, and therefore now we expected nothing but famine to perish at sea.

The sixteenth of October we made land, but we knew not what land it was. About sunset we put into a harbour, where we found a hulk of Dublin, and a pinnace of Hampton riding. Neither had we any boat to go ashore, until the pinnace sent off their boat to us with six or eight men, of whom we understood we were in Smerwick in the west parts of Ireland. They also relieved us presently with fresh water, wine, and other fresh meat. The eighteenth the governor and the master rode to Dingle five miles distant, to take order for the new victualling of our flyboat for England, and for relief of our sick and hurt men. But within four days after the boatswain, the steward, and the boatswain's mate died aboard the flyboat, and the twenty-eighth the master's mate and two of our chief sailors were brought sick to Dingle.

November the first the governor shipped himself in a ship called the *Monkey*, which was ready to put to sea for England, leaving the flyboat and all his company in Ireland. The same day we set sail, and on the third day we fell with the north side of the Land's End, and were shut up the Bristol Channel, but the next day we doubled the same for Mount's Bay. The fifth the Governor landed in England at Marazion, near Saint Michael's Mount in Cornwall.

The eighth we arrived at Southampton, where we understood that our consort the Admiral was come to Portsmouth, and had been there three weeks before. Ferdinandez, the master with his company, were not only come home without any prizes, but also in such weakness by sickness and death of their chiefest men, that they were scarce able to bring their ship into harbour; but were forced to let fall anchor without, which they could not weigh again, but might all have perished there if a small bark by great hap had not come to help them. *An. Dom.* 1587.

14

JOHN WHITE'S FIFTH VOYAGE, 1590

To the worshipful and my very friend Master Richard Hakluyt, much happiness in the Lord.

Sir, as well for the satisfying of your earnest request, as the performance of my promise made unto you at my last being with you in England, I have sent you (although in a homely style, especially for the contentation of a delicate ear) the true discourse of my last voyage into the West Indies, and parts of America called Virginia, taken in hand about the end of February, in the year of our redemption 1590. There were at the time three ships absolutely determined to go for the West Indies, at the special charges of Mr John Watts of London, merchant. But when they were fully furnished and in readiness to make their departure, a general stay was commanded of all ships throughout England. Which so soon as I heard, I acquainted Sir Walter Raleigh therewith, desiring him that, as I had sundry times before been chargeable and troublesome unto him for the supplies and reliefs of the planters in Virginia, so likewise that by his endeavour it would please him to procure licence for those three ships to proceed with their determined voyage. So that thereby the people in Virginia might speedily by comforted and relieved without further charges unto him. Whereupon he obtained licence of the Queen's Majesty. The owner of the three ships should be bound unto Sir Walter Raleigh or his assigns in 3000 pounds that those three ships in consideration of their release should transport a convenient number of passengers, with their furnitures and necessaries to be landed in Virginia. Nevertheless that order was not observed, neither was the bond taken according to the intention. But rather, in contempt of the order, I was by the owner and commanders of the ships denied to have any passengers, or anything else transported in any of the ships, saving only myself and my chest; no not so much as a boy to attend upon me. Notwithstanding, the scarcity of time was such that I could have no opportunity to go unto Sir Walter Raleigh with compalint; for the ships being then all in readiness to go to sea would have departed before I could return.

Thus both governors, masters, and sailors, regarding very smally the good of their countrymen in Virginia, determined nothing less than to touch at those places. They wholly disposed themselves to seek after prizes and spoils, spending so much time therein that summer was spent before we arrived at Virginia. When we were come thither, the season was so unfit and weather so foul that we were constrained of force to forsake that coast, having not seen any of our planters, with loss of one of our shipboats and seven of our chiefest men. And also with loss of three of our anchors and cables and most of our casks with fresh water left on shore. Which evils and unfortunate events had not chanced, if the order set down by Sir Walter Raleigh had been observed, or if my continual petitions for the performance of the same might have taken any place.

Thus may you plainly perceive the outcome of my fifth and last voyage to Virginia, which was no less unfortunately ended than forwardly begun, and as luckless to many as sinister to myself. But I would to God it had been as prosperous to all as noisome to the planters; and as joyful to me as discomfortable to them. Yet seeing it is not my first crossed voyage, I remain content. And, wanting my wishes, I leave off from prosecuring that whereunto I would to God my wealth were answerable to my will. Thus committing the relief of my discomfortable company, the planters in Virginia, to the merciful help of the Almighty, whom I most humbly beseech to help and comfort them, according to his most holy will and their good desire, I take my leave. From my house at Newtown in County Cork the fourth of February, 1593.

Your most well-wishing friend,

John White

The Fifth Voyage of Mr John White into the West Indies and parts of America called Virginia, in the year 1590.

The twentieth of March the three ships the *Hopewell, John Evangelist*, and the *Little John*, put to sea from Plymouth with two small shallops. The twenty-fifth at midnight both our shallops were sunk, being towed at the ships' sterns by the boatswain's negligence. On the thirtieth we saw ahead us that part of the coast of Barbary, lying east of Cape Cantin, and the Bay of Asphi. The next day we came to the isle of Mogador, where rode at our passing by a pinnace of London called the *Moonshine*.

On the first of April we anchored in Santa Cruz road, where we found two great ships of London lading in sugar, of whom we had two shipboats to supply the loss of our shallops. On the second we set sail from the road of Santa Cruz for the Canaries. On Saturday the fourth we saw Allegranza, the east isle of the Canaries. On Sunday the fifth of April we gave chase to a double flyboat; which we fought with and took her, with loss of three of their men slain and one hurt. On Monday the sixth we saw Grand Canary, and the next day we landed and took in fresh water on the south side thereof. On the ninth we departed from Grand Canary, and framed our course for Dominica.

The last of April we saw Dominica and came to anchor on the south side thereof. The first of May in the morning many of the savages came aboard our ships in their canoes and did traffic with us. We landed and entered their town, from whence we returned the same day aboard without any resistance of the savages, or any offence done to them. The second of May our Admiral and our pinnace departed from Dominica, leaving the *John* our Vice-admiral playing off and on about Dominica, hoping to take some Spaniard outward bound to the Indies. The same night we had sight of three small islands called Los Santos, leaving Guadaloupe and them on our starboard. The third we had sight of St Christopher's island, bearing northeast and by east off us.

On the fourth we sailed by the Virgins, which are many broken islands, lying at the east end of St John's island. The same day towards evening we landed upon one of them called Blanca, where we killed an incredible number of fowls. We stayed but three hours, and from thence stood into the shore north-west. Having brought this island south-east of us, we put towards night through an opening lying between the Virgins and the east end of St John. Here the pinnace left us and sailed on the south side of St John. The fifth and sixth the Admiral sailed along the north side of St John, so near the shore that the Spaniards discerned us to be men-of-war; and therefore made fires along the coast as we sailed by, for so their custom is when they see any men-of-war on their coasts. The seventh we landed on the north-west end of St John, where we watered in a good river called Yaguana. The same night following we took a frigate of ten tons coming from Gwathanelo laden with hides and ginger. In this place Pedro, a mulatto, who knew all our state, ran from us to the Spaniards. On the ninth we departed from Yaguana.

The thirteenth we landed on an island called Mona, whereon were 10 or 12 houses inhabited of the Spaniards. These we burned and took from them a pinnace, which they had drawn aground and sunk, and carried all her sails, masts and rudders into the woods, because we should not take her away. We also chased the Spaniards over all the island; but they hid them in caves, hollow rocks and bushes, so that we could not find them. On the fourteenth we departed from Mona. The next day we came to an island called Saona, about five leagues distant from Mona, lying on the south side of Hispaniola near the east end. Between these two islands we lay off and on four or five days, hoping to take some of the Santo Domingo fleet doubling this island, as nearer way to Spain than by Cape Tiburon, or by Cape St Anthony.

On Thursday being the nineteenth, our Vice-admiral from which we departed at Dominica, came to us at Saona, with which we left a Spanish frigate, and appointed him to lie off and on another five days between Saona and Mona to the end aforesaid. Then we departed from them at Saona for Cape Tiburon. Here I was informed that our men of the Vice-admiral, at their departure from Dominica, brought away two young savages, who were the chief Casique's sons of that country and part of Dominica. But they shortly after ran away from them at Santa Cruz island, where the Vice-admiral landed to take in ballast.

On the twenty-first the Admiral came to Cape Tiburon, where we found the *John Evangelist* our pinnace staying for us. Here we took in two Spaniards almost starved on the shore, who made a fire to our ships as we passed by. Those places for an hundred miles in length are nothing else but a desolate wilderness, without any habitation of people, and full of wild bulls and boars and great serpents.

The twenty-second our pinnace came also to anchor in Aligato Bay at Cape Tiburon. Here we understood of Mr Lane, captain of the pinnace, how he was set upon by one of the king's galleys belonging to Santo Domingo, which was manned by four hundred men. After he had fought with him three or four hours they gave over the fight and forsook him, without any great hurt done on either part. The twenty-sixth the *John*, our Vice-admiral, came to us to Cape Tiburon, and the frigate which we left with him at Saona. This was the appointed place where we should attend for the meeting with the Santo Domingo fleet. On Whitsunday even at Cape Tiburon one of our boys ran away from us, and at ten days' end returned to our ships almost starved for want of food. In sundry places about this part of Cape Tiburon we found the bones and carcases of divers men, who had perished (as we thought) by famine in those woods, being either straggled from their company, or landed there by some men-of-war.

On the fourteenth of June we took a small Spanish frigate which fell amongst us so suddenly, as he doubled the point at the bay of Cape Tiburon where we rode that he could not escape us. This frigate came from Santo Domingo and had but three men in her. The one was an expert pilot, the other a mountaineer, and the third a vintner, who escaped all out of prison at Santo Domingo, purposing to fly to Yaguana: a town in the west parts of Hispaniola where many fugitive Spaniards are gathered together. The seventeenth being Wednesday captain Lane was sent to Yaguana with his pinnace and a frigate to take a ship, which was there taking in freight, as we understood by the old pilot whom we had taken three days before. The twenty-fourth the frigate returned from captain Lane at Yaguana, and brought us word to Cape Tiburon that he had taken the ship, with many passengers and negroes in the same. This proved not so rich a prize as we hoped for; for a French man-of-war had taken and spoiled her before we came. Nevertheless her loading was thought worth 1000 or 1300 pounds, being hides, ginger, cannafistula, copper-pans, and cassavi.

The second July Edward Spicer, whom we left in England, came to us at Cape Tiburon, accompanied with a small pinnace, whereof one Mr Harps was captain. The same day we had sight of a fleet of fourteen sail all of Santo Domingo, to whom we immediately gave chase. But they upon the first sight of us fled, and separating themselves scattered here and there. Wherefore we were forced to divide ourselves and so made after them until twelve o'clock of the night. But then by reason of the darkness we lost sight of each other. Yet in the end the Admiral and the *Moonshine* happened to be together the same night at the fetching up of the Vice-admiral of the Spanish fleet. Against whom the next morning we fought and took him, with loss of one of our men and two hurt, and of theirs' four slain and six hurt. But what was become of our Vice-admiral, our pinnace, and prize, and two frigates in all this time we were ignorant. The third of July we spent about rifling, rummaging and fitting the prize to be sailed by us. The sixth of July we saw Jamaica, which we left on our larboard, keeping Cuba in sight on our starboard.

Upon the eighth of July we saw the island of Pinos, which lies on the south side of Cuba nigh unto the west end called Cape St Anthony. The same day we gave chase to a frigate, but at night we lost sight of her, partly by the slow sailing of our Admiral, and lack of the *Moonshine* our pinnace, which Captain Cooke had sent to the cape the day before. On the eleventh we came to Cape St Anthony, where we found our consort the *Moonlight* and her pinnace abiding for our coming. We understood that the day before there passed by them twenty-two sail, some of them of the burden of 300 and some

400 tons, laden with the king's treasure from the mainland, bound for Havana. From this eleventh of July until the twenty-second we were much becalmed; the wind being very scarce and the weather exceeding hot, we were much pestered with the Spaniards we had taken. Wherefore we were driven to land all the Spaniards saving three; the place their own choice on the south side of Cuba, near unto the Organos and Rio de Puercos.

The twenty-third we had sight of the cape of Florida, and the broken islands thereof called the Martires. The twenty-fifth being St James's day in the morning, we fell with the Matanças, a headland eight leagues towards the east of Havana, where we purposed to take fresh water in, and make our abode two or three days. On Sunday the twenty-sixth of July, plying to and fro between the Matanças and Havana, we were espied by three small pinnaces of St John de Ulloa bound for Havana, which were exceeding richly laden. These three pinnaces came very boldly up unto us, and so continued until they came within musket shot of us. We supposed them to be captain Harps' pinnace and two small frigates taken by him; whereupon we showed our flag.

But they immediately upon the sight of it turned about and made all the sail they could from us toward the shore. They kept themselves in so shallow water that we were not able to follow them, and therefore gave them over with expense of shot and powder to no purpose. If we had not so rashly set out our flag, we might have taken them all three; for they would not have known us before they had been in our hands. This chase brought us so far to leeward as Havana. Wherefore not finding any of our consorts at Matanças, we put over again to the cape of Florida and from thence through the channel of Bahama. On the twenty-eighth the cape of Florida bore west of us. The thirtieth we lost sight of the coast of Florida, and stood to sea to gain the help of the current which runs much swifter afar off than in sight of the coast. For from the cape to Virginia all along the shore are none but eddy currents, setting to the south and south-west. The thirty-first our three ships were clear of them, the great prize, the Admiral, and the *Moonlight*; but our prize departed from us without taking leave of our Admiral or consort, and sailed directly for England.

On the first of August the wind scanted. Thenceforward we had very foul weather and very much rain, thundering, and great spouts which fell round about us night unto our ships. The third we stood again in for the shore, and at midday we took the height of the same. The height of that place we found to be 34 degrees of latitude. Towards night we were within three leagues of the low sandy islands west of Wokokon. But the weather continued so exceeding foul that we could not anchor nigh the coast. Wherefore we stood off again to sea until Monday the ninth of August.

On Monday the storm ceased, and we had very great likelihood of fair weather. Therefore we stood in again for the shore, and came to anchor at eleven fathoms in 35 degrees of latitutde, within a mile of the shore. We went on land on the narrow sandy island, one of those west of Wokokon. Here we took in some fresh water and caught great store of fish in the shallow water. Between the mainland (as we supposed) and that island was but a mile over, and three or four foot deep in most places. On the twelfth in the morning we departed and toward night we came to anchor at the north-east end of the island of Croatoan, by reason of a breach which we perceived to lie out two or three leagues into the sea. Here we rode all that night.

The thirteenth in the morning before we weighed our anchors, our boats were sent to sound over this breach. Our ships riding on the side thereof at five fathoms; a ship's length from us we found but four and a quarter. Then deepening and shallowing for the space of two miles, so that sometimes we found five fathoms, and by and by seven; within two casts with the lead nine, then eight; next cast five, then six, then four, and then nine again, and deeper. But three fathoms was the last, two leagues off from the shore. This breach is in 35 degrees and a half, and lies at the very north-east point of Croatoan, whereat goes a fret out of the main sea into the inner waters, which part the islands and the mainland. The fifteenth of August towards evening we came to anchor at Hatorask, in 36 degrees and one third, in five fathoms water, three leagues from the shore. At our first coming to this shore we saw a great smoke rise in the isle of Roanoke near the place where I left our Colony in the year 1587. This put us in good hope that some of the Colony were there expecting my return out of England.

The sixteenth and next morning our two boats went ashore, and captain Cocke, and captain Spicer, and their company with me, with intent to pass to the place at Roanoke where our countrymen were left. At our putting from the ship we commanded our master gunner to make ready two minions and a falcon well loaded, and to shoot them off with reasonable space between every shot, to the end that their reports might be heard to the place where we hoped to find some of our people. This was accordingly performed; our two boats put unto the shore, in the Admiral's boat we sounded all the way and found from our ship until we came within a mile of the shore nine, eight, and seven fathoms. But before we were half way between our ships and the shore we saw another great smoke to the south-west of Kenrick's Mounts; we therefore thought good to go to that second smoke first.

But it was much further from the harbour where we landed than we supposed it to be; so that we were very sore tired before we came to the smoke. But that which grieved us more was that, when we came to the smoke we found no man nor sign that any had been there lately, nor yet any fresh water in all this way to drink. Being thus wearied with this journey we returned to the harbour where we left our boats, who in our absence had brought their cask ashore for fresh water. So we deferred our going to Roanoke until the next morning, and caused some of those sailors to dig in those sandy hills for fresh water: whereof we found very sufficient. That night we returned aboard with our boats and our whole company in safety.

The next morning, the seventeenth of August, our boats and company were prepared again to go up to Roanoke. But captain Spicer had then sent his boat ashore for fresh water, by means whereof it was ten of the clock aforenoon before we put from our ships, which were then come to anchor within two miles of the shore. The Admiral's boat was halfway toward the shore when captain Spicer put off from his ship. The Admiral's boat first passed the breach, but not without some danger of sinking; for a sea broke into our boat which filled us half full of water. But by the will of God and careful steerage of captain Cocke, we came safe ashore, saving only that our furniture, victuals, match and powder were much wet and spoiled. For the wind blew at north-east and direct into the harbour so great a gale, that the sea broke extremely on the bar, and the tide went very forcibly at the entrance.

By that time our Admiral's boat was hauled ashore, and most of our things taken out to dry, captain Spicer came to the entrance of the breach with his mast standing up, and was half passed over. But by the rash and indiscreet steerage of Ralph Skinner, his master's mate, a very dangerous sea broke into their boat and overset them quite. The men kept the boat, some in it and some hanging on it; but the next sea set the boat on ground, where it beat so, that some of them were forced to let go their hold, hoping to wade ashore. But the sea still beat them down, so that they could neither stand nor swim. The boat twice or thrice was turned the keel upward; whereon captain Spicer and Skinner hung until they sank, and were seen no more. But four that could swim a little kept themselves in deeper water and were saved by captain Cocke's means; who, so soon as he saw their oversetting, stripped himself and four others that could swim very well, and with all haste possible rowed unto them, and saved four. They were eleven in all, and seven of the chiefest were drowned.

This mischance did so much discomfort the sailors that they were all of one mind not to go any further to seek the planters. But in the end by the commandment and persuasion of me and captain Cocke, they prepared the boats; and seeing the captain and me so resolute, they seemed much more willing. Our boats and all things fitted again, we put off from Hatorask, nineteen persons in both boats. But before we could get to the place where our planters were left, it was so exceeding dark that we overshot the place a quarter of a mile. There we spied towards the north end of the island the light of a great fire through the woods, to which we presently rowed. When we came right over against it, we let fall our grapnel near the shore and sounded with a trumpet a call, and afterwards many familiar English tunes of songs, and called to them friendly. But we had no answer; we therefore landed at day-break, and coming to the fire, we found the grass and sundry rotten trees burning about the place.

From hence we went through the woods to that part of the island directly over against Dasamonquepeio. Thence we returned by the waterside round about the north point of the island, until we came to the place where I left our Colony in the year 1586. In all this way we saw in the sand the print of the savages' feet of two or three sorts trodden the night. As we entered up the sandy bank upon a tree, in the very brow thereof, were curiously carved these fair Roman letters C R O. These letters we knew to signify the place where I should find the planters seated, according to a secret token agreed upon between them and me at my last departure from them. This was that in any way they should not fail to write or carve on the trees or posts of the doors the name of the place where they should be seated. For at my coming away they were prepared to remove from Roanoke fifty miles into the mainland. Therefore at my departure in anno 1587 I willed them that, if they should happen to be distressed in any of those places, they should carve over the letters or name a cross + in this form. But we found no such sign of distress.

Having well considered of this, we passed toward the place where they were left in sundry houses. But we found the houses taken down, and the place very strongly enclosed with a high palisade of great trees, with curtains and flankers very fort-like. One of the chief trees or posts at the right side of the entrance had the bark taken off, and five foot from the ground in fair capital letters was graven CROATOAN without any cross or signal of distress. We entered into the palisade, where we found many bars of iron, two pigs of lead, four iron fowlers, iron saker-shot, and such like heavy things thrown here and there, almost overgrown with grass and weeds. Thence we went along by the waterside towards the point of the creek to see if we could find any of their boats or pinnace, but we could perceive no sign of them, nor any of the last falcons and small ordnance which were left with them.

At our return from the creek some of our sailors told us

that they had found where divers chests had been hidden, and long since digged up again and broken up. Much of the goods in them was spoiled and scattered about, but nothing left of such things as the savages knew any use of undefaced. Captain Cocke and I went to the place, which was in the end of an old trench made two years past by captain Amadas. We found five chests, that had been carefully hidden by the planters, and of the same chests three were my own. About the place were many of my things spoiled and broken, my books torn from the covers, the frames of some of my pictures and maps rotten and spoiled with rain, and my armour almost eaten through with rust.

This could be no other but the deed of the savages our enemies at Dadamonquepeio, who had watched the departure of our men to Croatoan; and as soon as they departed, digged up every place where they suspected anything to be buried. But although it much grieved me to see such spoil of my goods, yet on the other side I greatly joyed that I had found a certain token of their safe being at Croatoan, which is the place where Manteo was born and the savages of the island our friends.

When we had seen in this place so much as we could, we returned to our boats, and departed from the shore towards our ships with as much speed as we could. For the weather began to overcast, and very likely that a foul and stormy night would ensue. Therefore the same evening with much danger and labour we got ourselves aboard; by which time the wind and seas were so greatly risen that we doubted our cables and anchors would scarcely hold until morning. Wherefore the captain caused the boat to be manned with five lusty men who could swim all well, and sent them to the little island on the right hand of the harbour, to bring aboard six of our men, who had filled our cask with fresh water. The boat the same night returned aboard with our men, but all our cask ready filled they left behind: impossible to be had aboard without danger of casting away both men and boats; for this night proved very stormy and foul.

Next morning it was agreed by the captain and myself, with the master and others, to weigh anchor and go for the place at Croatoan, where our planters were. For then the wind was good for that place, and also to leave that cask with fresh water on shore in the island until our return. So then they brought the cable to the captain, but when the anchor was almost up the cable broke. Thus we lost another anchor, wherewith we drove so fast into the shore that we were forced to let fall a third anchor. This came so fast home that the ship was almost aground by Kenrick's Mounts. So that we were forced to let slip the cable end for end. And if it had not chanced that we had fallen into a channel of deeper water, closer by the shore than we accounted for, we could never have gone clear of the point that lies to the southward of Kenrick's Mounts.

Being thus clear of some dangers and gotten into deeper waters, but not without some loss – for we had but one cable and anchor left us of four, and the weather grew to be fouler and fouler; our victuals scarce and our cask and fresh water lost – it was therefore determined that we should go to Saint John or some other island to the southward for fresh water. If we could any ways supply our wants of victuals and other necessaries, at Hispaniola, Saint John, or Trinidad, then we should continue in the Indies all the winter following, with hope to make two rich voyages of one, and at our return to visit our countrymen at Virginia. The captain and the whole company in the Admiral (with my earnest petitions) thereunto agreed; so that it rested only to know what the master of the *Moonlight* our consort would be herein. But when we demanded if they would accompany us they alleged that their weak and leaky ship was not able to continue it. Wherefore the same night we parted, leaving the *Moonlight* to go directly for England, and the Admiral set his course for Trinidad: which course we kept two days.

On the twenty-eighth the wind changed, and it was set on foul weather every way. This storm brought the wind west and north-west, and blew so forcibly that we were able to bear no sail, but our fore-course half mast high. So we ran upon the wind perforce the due course for England. We were driven to change our first determination for Trinidad, and stood for the islands of Azores, where we purposed to take in fresh water: and also there hoped to meet with some English men-of-war at whose hands we might obtain some supply of our wants. Thus continuing our course for the Azores, sometimes with calms and sometimes with very scarce winds, on the fifteenth of September the wind came south south-east, and blew so exceedingly that we were forced to hove to all that day. By account we judged ourselves to be about twenty leagues to the west of Corvo and Flores. About night the storm ceased and fair weather ensued.

On Thursday the seventeenth we saw Corvo and Flores, but we could not come to anchor that night, by reason the wind shifted. The next morning being the eighteenth, standing in again with Corvo, we escried a sail ahead us, to whom we gave chase. When we came near him we knew him to be a Spaniard, and hoped to make sure capture of him; but we understood at our speaking with him that he was a prize, and of the Domingo fleet already taken by the *John*, our consort, in the Indies. We learned also of this prize that our Vice-admiral and pinnace had fought with the rest of the Domingo fleet, and had forced them with their Admiral to flee unto Jamaica under the Fort for succour. Some of them ran themselves aground; whereof one of them they brought away, and took out of some others so much as the time would permit.

In their return from Jamaica about the Organos near Cape Saint Anthony, our Vice-admiral met with two ships of the mainland, come from Mexico bound for Havana, with whom he fought. Our Vice-admiral's lieutenant was slain, and the captain's right arm struck off, with four others of his men slain and sixteen hurt. But in the end he entered, and took one of the Spanish ships, which was so sore shot by us under water that before they could take out her treasure she sank. So that we lost thirteen pipes of silver which sank with her, besides much other rich merchandise. In the meantime the other Spanish ship, being pierced with nine shot under water, got away; which our Vice-admiral intended to pursue. But some of their men in the top made certain rocks, which they saw above water near the shore, to be galleys of Havana and Cartagena, coming from Havana to rescue the two ships. Wherefore they gave over their chase, and went for England. After this intelligence was given us by this our prize, he departed from us and went for England.

On Saturday, the nineteenth of September, we came to anchor near a small village on the north side of Flores. Here we found riding five English men-of-war, of whom we understood that our Vice-admiral and prize were gone thence for England. One of these five was the *Moonlight*, our consort, which upon the first sight of our coming into Flores set sail and went for England, not taking any leave of us.

On Sunday the twentieth the *Mary Rose*, Admiral of the Queen's fleet, wherein was general Sir John Hawkins, stood in with Flores; and divers others of the Queen's ships, the *Hope*, the *Nonpareil*, the *Rainbow*, the *Swift-sure*, the *Foresight*, with many other good merchant ships-of-war, as the *Edward Bonaventure*, the *Merchant Royal*, the *Amity*, the *Eagle*, the *Dainty* of Sir John Hawkins, and many other good ships and pinnaces, all attending to meet with the king of Spain's fleet coming from *Terra firma* of the West Indies.

The twenty-second of September we went aboard the *Rainbow*, and towards night we spoke with the *Swift-sure*, and gave him three pieces. The captains desired our company; wherefore we willingly attended on them: who at this time with ten other ships stood for Fayal. But the general with the rest of the fleet were separated from us, making two fleets, for the surer meeting with the Spanish fleet. On Wednesday the twenty-third we saw Graciosa, where the Admiral and the rest of the Queen's fleet were come together. The Admiral put forth a flag of counsel, in which was determined that the whole fleet should go for the mainland, and spread themselves on the coasts of Spain and Portugal, so far as conveniently they might, for the surer meeting of the Spanish fleet in those parts. The twenty-sixth we came to Fayal, where the Admiral with some others of the fleet anchored, others plied up and down between that and Pico until midnight. Then the *Antony* shot off a piece and weighed, showing his light; after whom the whole fleet stood to the east, the wind at north-east by east.

On Sunday the twenty-seventh towards evening we took our leave of the Admiral and the whole fleet, which stood to the east. But our ship accompanied with a flyboat stood in again with St George, where we purposed to take in more fresh water, and some other fresh victuals. On Wednesday the thirtieth of September, seeing the wind hang so northerly that we could not attain the island of St George, we gave over our purpose to water there, and the next day framed our due course for England. The second of October in the morning we saw St Michael's island on our starboard quarter. The twenty-third at ten of the clock before noon, we saw Ushant in Brittany. On Saturday the twenty-fourth we came in safety, God be thanked, to anchor at Plymouth.

15

HAKLUYT ON THE FRENCH AND SPANIARDS IN NORTH AMERICA

To the right honourable Sir Walter Raleigh, knight, Captain of her Majesty's Guard, Lord Warden of the Stannaries, and her Highness' Lieutenant-general of the County of Cornwall, R.H. wishes true felicity.

Sir, after this history [of Florida] was lately published in France under your name by my learned friend, M. Martin Basanier of Paris, I was easily induced to turn it into English, understanding that the same was no less grateful to you here than I know it to be acceptable to many great and worthy persons there. And no marvel it were very welcome unto you, and that you liked the translation thereof, since no history hitherto set forth has more affinity, resemblance or conformity with yours of Virginia than this of Florida.

But calling to mind that you had spent more years in France than I, and understand French better than myself, I perceived that you approved my endeavour, not for any private commodity that thereby might redound unto you, but that it argued a singular and especial care you had of those who are to be employed in your own like enterprise. By the reading of this my translation you would have forewarned them to beware of the gross negligence in providing of sufficiency of victuals, the security, disorders, and mutinies that fell out among the French, with the great inconveniences that thereupon ensured. By others' mishaps they might learn to prevent and avoid the like. They also might be put in mind by reading of the manifold commodities and great fertility of the places described, so near neighbours unto our Colonies, that they might be awaked and stirred up unto the diligent observation of everything that might turn to the advancement of the action, whereinto they are so cheerfully entered.

Many special points concerning the commodities of these parts, the accidents of the Frenchmen's government therein, the causes of their good or bad success, with the occasions of the abandoning one of their forts and the surprise of the other by the enemy, are herein truly and faithfully recorded. The same with divers other things of chiefest importance are lively drawn in colours at your no small charges by the skilful painter James Morgues, sometime living in the Blackfriars in London (whom Monsieur Châtillon, then admiral of France, sent thither with Laudonnière for that purpose) who was an eye-witness of the goodness and fertility of those regions.

These four voyages I knew not to whom I might better offer than to yourself, for divers just considerations. First, for they were dedicated unto you in French. Secondly, because now four times also you have attempted the like upon the selfsame coast near adjoining. Thirdly, in that you have pierced as far up into the mainland and discovered no less secrets in the parts of your abode than the French did in the places of their inhabiting. Lastly, considering you are now also ready (upon the late return of captain Stafford and good news which he brought you of the safe arrival of your last Colony in their wished haven) to prosecute this action more thoroughly than ever.

Your enterprise, I affirm, if the same may speedily and effectually be pursued, will prove far more beneficial in divers respects unto this realm than the world, yea many of the wiser sort, have hitherto imagined. The particular commodities whereof are well known unto yourself and some few others, and are faithfully committed to writing by one of your followers, who remained there about a twelvemonth with your worshipful lieutenant Mr Ralph Lane, in the diligent search of the secrets of those countries. Touching the speedy and effectual pursuing of your action, though I know well it would demand a prince's purse to have it thoroughly followed without lingering, yet am I of opinion that you shall draw the same before long to be profitable and gainful as well to those of our nation there remaining, as to the merchants of

England that shall trade hereafter thither. Partly by certain secret commodities already discovered by your servants, and partly be breeding divers sorts of beasts in those large and ample regions, and planting such things in that warm climate as will best prosper there, and our realm stand most in need of.

This I find to have been the course that both the Spaniards and Portuguese took in the beginnings of their discoveries and conquests. The Spaniards at their first entrance into Hispaniola found neither sugar-canes nor ginger growing there, nor any kind of our cattle. But finding the place fit for pasture, they sent cows and bulls and sundry sorts of other profitable beasts thither, and transported the plants of sugar-canes, and set the roots of ginger. The hides of which oxen, with sugar and ginger, are now the chief merchandise of that island. The Portuguese also at their footing in Madeira found nothing there but mighty woods for timber; whereupon they called the island by that name. Howbeit the climate being favourable, they enriched it by their own industry with the best wines and sugars in the world. The like manner of proceeding they used in the isles of the Azores by sowing therein great quantity of woad. So dealt they in St Thomas under the equinoctial, and in Brazil, and sundry other places.

If our men will follow their steps by your wise direction, I doubt not but in due time they shall reap no less commodity and benefit. Moreover there is none other likelihood but that her Majesty, who has christened and given the name to your Virginia, if need require, will deal after the manner of honourable godmothers, who, seeing their gossips not fully able to bring up their children themselves, are wont to contribute to their honest education, the rather if they find any towardliness or reasonable hope of goodness in them.

The mainland, where your last Colony mean to seat themselves, is replenished with many thousands of Indians, who are of better wits than those of Mexico and Peru, as has been found by those that have had some trial of them; whereby it may be gathered that they will easily embrace the Gospel, forsaking their idolatry . . . Now if the greatness of the mainland of Virginia and the large extension thereof, especially to the west, should make you think that the subduing of it were a matter of more difficulty than the conquest of Ireland, first I answer, that – as the late experience of that skilful pilot and captain Mr John Davis to the north-west (toward his discovery yourself have thrice contributed with the forwardest) has showed a great part to be main sea, where before was thought to be main land – so for my part I am fully persuaded by Ortelius' late reformation of Culuacan and the gulf of California that the land on the back part of Virginia extends nothing so far westward as is put down in the maps of those parts.

Moreover, it is not to be denied but that one hundred men will do more now, among the naked and unarmed people in Virginia than one thousand were able to do in Ireland against that armed and warlike nation in those days [of Strongbow]. I say further that these two years' last experience has plainly showed that we may spare 10,000 able men without any miss. Seeing therefore we are so far from want of people that, retiring daily home out of the Low Countries they go idly up and down in swarms for lack of honest entertainment, I see no fitter place to employ some part of the better sort of them trained up thus long in service, than in the inward parts of Virginia against such stubborn savages as shall refuse obedience to her Majesty. From London the first of May 1587.

Your lordship's humble at commandment,

R. Hakluyt

16

SIR FRANCIS DRAKE IN CALIFORNIA,
1578

The course which Sir Francis Drake held from the haven of Guatulco in the South Sea on the back side of Nueva España to the north-west of California as far as 43 degrees; and his return back along the said coast to 38 degrees. Where, finding a fair and goodly haven, he landed and, staying there many weeks and discovering many excellent things in the country and great show of rich mineral matter, and being offered the dominion of the country by the lord of the same, he took possession thereof on behalf of her Majesty and named it Nova Albion.

We kept our course from the isle of Cano (which lies in eight degrees of northerly latitude, and within two leagues of the mainland of Nicaragua, where we caulked and trimmed our ship) along the coast of Nueva España, until we came to the haven and town of Guatulco, which (as we were informed) had but seventeen Spaniards dwelling in it. We found it to stand in 15 degrees and 50 minutes. As soon as we entered this haven we landed, and went presently to the town, and to the town house, where we found a judge sitting in judgement, with three other officers, upon three negroes that had conspired the burning of the town. Both judges and prisoners we took, and brought them on shipboard, and caused the chief judge to write his letter to the town, to command all the townsmen to vacate, that we might safely water there. When they departed, we ransacked the town. In one house we found a pot of the quantity of a bushel, full of rials of plate, which we brought to our ship. And here one Thomas Moon, one of our company, took a Spanish gentleman as he was flying out of the town; searching him, he found a chain of gold about him and other jewels, which we took and so let him go. At this place our general, among other Spaniards set ashore his Portuguese pilot, whom he took at the island of Cape Verde, out of a ship of Saint Mary port of Portugal. Having set them ashore, we departed thence. Our general at this place and time – thinking himself both in respect of his private injuries received from the Spaniards, as also of their contempts and indignities offered to our country and prince in general, sufficiently satisfied and revened – purposed to continue no longer upon the Spanish coasts, but began to consider the best way for his country.

He thought it not good to return by the straits, for two special causes. The one, lest the Spaniards should there wait for him in great number and strength; whose hands he, being left but one ship, could not possibly escape. The other cause was the dangerous situation of the mouth of the Straits on the south side, with continual storms, as he found by experience, besides the shoals and sands upon the coast. Wherefore he thought it not a good course to adventure that way. He resolved therefore to go forward to the isles of the Moluccas, and therehence to sail the course of the Portuguese by the cape of Good Hope.

Upon this resulution he began to think of his best way for the Moluccas. Finding himself, where he now was, becalmed, he saw that of necessity he must be enforced to take a Spanish course, namely to sail somewhat northerly to get a wind. We therefore set sail and sailed eight hundred leagues at the least for a good wind – from the sixteenth of April after our old style till the third of June.

The fifth day of June, being in 43 degrees toward the pole Arctic, being speedily come out of the extreme heat, we found the air so cold that our men complained of the extremity thereof. The further we went the more cold increased upon us. Whereupon we thought it best to seek land and did so; finding it not mountainous but low plain land. We drew back again without landing till we came within 38 degrees towards the Line. In which height it pleased God to send us into a fair and good bay with a good wind to enter.

In this bay we anchored the seventeenth of June. The people

of the country, having their houses close by the water's side, showed themselves unto us and sent a present to our general. When they came unto us they greatly wondered at the things which we brought. Our general (according to his natural and accustomed humanity) courteously entreated them, and liberally bestowed on them necessary things to cover their nakedness. Whereupon they supposed us to be gods, and would not be persuaded to the contrary. The presents which they sent unto our general were feathers, and cauls of net work.

Their houses are digged round about with earth, and have from the uttermost brims of the circle clefts of wood set upon them, joining close together at the top like a spire steeple, which by reason of that closeness are very warm. Their bed is the ground with rushes strewed on it and lying about the house; they have the fire in the midst. The men go naked; the women take bulrushes and comb them after the manner of hemp, and thereof make their loose garments; which, being knit about their middles, hang down about their hips, having also about their shoulders a skin of deer, with the hair upon it. These women are very obedient and serviceable to their husbands.

They came and visited us the second time, and brought with them feathers and bags of tobacco for presents. When they came to the top of the hill (at the bottom whereof we had pitched our tents) they stayed. One, appointed for speaker, wearied himself with making a long oration; which done, they left their bows upon the hill and came down with their presents.

In the meantime the women remaining on the hill tormented themselves lamentably, tearing their flesh from their cheeks, whereby we perceived that they were about a sacrifice. In the meantime our general with his company went to prayer and to reading of the Scriptures. At which exercise they were attentive and seemed greatly to be affected with it. But when they were come unto us they restored again unto us those things which before we had bestowed upon them.

The news of our being there being spread through the country, the people that inhabited round about came down; amongst them the king himself, a man of a goodly stature and comely personage, with many other tall and warlike men. Before whose coming were sent two ambassadors to our general to signify that their king was coming; in doing of which message their speech was continued about half an hour. This ended, they by signs requested our general to send something by their hand to their king, as a token that his coming might be in peace. Wherein our general having satisfied them, they returned with glad tidings to their king. He marched to us with a princely majesty, the people crying continually after their manner; as they drew near unto us, so did they strive to behave themselves in their actions with comeliness.

In the forefront was a man of a goodly personage, who bore the sceptre or mace before the king, whereupon hanged two crowns, a less and a bigger, with three chains of a marvellous length. The crowns were made of knit work wrought artificially with feathers of divers colours; the chains were made of a bony substance. Few be the persons among them that are admitted to wear them; of that number also the persons are stinted, as some ten, some twelve, &c. Next unto him who bore the sceptre was the king himself with his guard about his person, clad with coney and other skins. After them followed the naked common sort of people, every one having his face painted, some with white, some with black and other colours, having in their hands one thing or other for a present, not so much as their children but they also brought their presents.

In the meantime our general gathered his men together and marched within his fenced place, making against their approaching a very warlike show. They being trooped together in their order and a general salutation being made, there was presently a general silence. Then he that bore the sceptre before the king, being informed by another, with a manly and lofty voice proclaimed that which the other spoke to him in secret, continuing half an hour. Which ended, and a general Amen as it were given, the king with the whole number of men and women (the children excepted) came down without any weapon; who descending to the foot of the hill set themselves in order.

In coming towards our bulwarks and tents the sceptre

bearer began a song, observing his measures in a dance, and that with a stately countenance. The king with his guard and every degree of persons following did in like manner sing and dance, saving only the women who danced and kept silence. The general permitted them to enter within our bulwark, where they continued their song and dance a reasonable time. When they had satisfied themselves, they made signs to our general to sit down; to whom the king and divers others made several orations, or rather supplication, that he would take their province and kingdom into his hand and become their king. They made signs that they would resign unto him their right and title of the whole land and become his subjects.

To persuade us the better the king and the rest, with one consent and with great reverence, joyfully singing a song, did set the crown upon his head, enriched his neck with all their chains and offered unto him many other things, honouring him by the name of Hioh, adding thereunto a sign of triumph. Our general thought not meet to reject it because he knew not what honour and profit it might be to our country. Wherefore in the name and to the use of her Majesty, he took the sceptre, crown and dignity of the said country in his hands, wishing that the riches and treasure thereof might so conveniently be transported to the enriching of her kingdom at home, as it abound in the same.

The common sort of the people, leaving the king and his guard with our general, scattered themselves together with their sacrifices among our people, taking a diligent view of every person. Such as pleased their fancy (who were the youngest), they, enclosing them about, offered their sacrifices unto them with lamentable weeping, scratching, and tearing the flesh from their faces with their nails, whereof issued abundance of blood. But we used signs to them of disliking this, stayed their hands from force, and directed them upwards to the living God, whom only they ought to worship. They showed unto us their wounds, and craved help of them at our hands; whereupon we gave them lotions, plasters and ointments agreeing to the state of their griefs, beseeching God to cure their diseases.

Every third day they brought their sacrifices unto us, until they understood our meaning, that we had no pleasure in them. Yet they could not be long absent from us, but daily frequented our company to the hour of our departure, which seemed so grievous unto them that their joy was turned into sorrow. They entreated us that being absent we would remember them and by stealth provided a sacrifice, which we misliked.

Our necessary business ended, our general with his company travelled up into the country to their villages; where we found herds of deer by a thousand in a company, being most large and fat of body. We found the whole country to be a warren of a strange kind of conies, their bodies in bigness as be the Barbary conies, their heads as the heads of ours, the feet of a mole, and the tail of a rat being of great length. Under her chin on either side a bag into the which she gathers her meat when she has filled her belly abroad. The people eat their bodies and make great account of their skins, for their king's coat was made of them.

Our general called this country New Albion, for two causes: the one in respect of the white banks and cliffs, which lie towards the sea; and the other, because it might have some affinity with our country in name, which sometime was so called. There is no part of earth here to be taken up, wherein there is not some special likelihood of gold or silver. At our departure hence our general set up a monument of our being there; as also of her Majesty's right and title to the same, namely a plate nailed upon a fair great post, whereupon was engraven her Majesty's name, the day and year of our arrival there, with the free given up of the province and people into her Majesty's hands; together with her Highness' picture and arms in a piece of sixpence of current English money under the plate, where under was also written the name of our general.

It seems that the Spaniards hitherto had never been in this part of the country, neither did ever discover the land by many degrees to the southwards of this place.